SOTHIS PRESS

Sothis Press aims to completely reimagine the public domain book with an emphasis on universal access to captivatingly designed print editions. We believe that technology will enable every single book ever published to be perpetually accessible in beautiful print form. Sothis is beauty in ubiquity.

www.sothis.press
1 Waterhouse Square, London, ECIN 2ST

Livermore's Trustees' Handbook

A Manual for the Use of Trustees, Executors, Administrators, Assignees for the Benefit of Creditors, Receivers, Guardians, and Committees of Lunatics, Idiots, and Habitual Drunkards, Containing a Brief Statement of Their Powers and Duties, Rights and Liab

Rufus P. Livermore

SOTHIS PRESS

ISBN 978-1-0368-0780-1

Livermore's Trustees' Handbook
is in the public domain.

This edition is published by
Sothis Press © 2023. The company
is registered in England and Wales.
The Company Number is 14900389.

LIVERMORE'S

TRUSTEES' HANDBOOK;

A MANUAL

FOR THE USE OF

TRUSTEES, EXECUTORS, ADMINISTRATORS, ASSIGNEES FOR THE BENEFIT OF CREDITORS, RECEIVERS, GUARDIANS, AND COMMITTEES OF LUNATICS, IDIOTS, AND HABITUAL DRUNKARDS.

CONTAINING

A BRIEF STATEMENT OF THEIR POWERS AND DUTIES, RIGHTS AND LIABILITIES, WITH PRACTICAL SUGGESTIONS AND INFORMATION FOR THEIR GUIDANCE IN THE MANAGEMENT OF THEIR TRUSTS GENERALLY, AND PARTICULARLY AS TO MATTERS RELATING TO THEIR ACCOUNTS, AND THE SETTLEMENT OF THEM, UPON THEIR APPLICATION TO BE DISCHARGED.

BY

RUFUS P. LIVERMORE,

OF THE NEW YORK BAR.

NEW YORK:

L. K. STROUSE & CO., PUBLISHERS,

95 NASSAU STREET.

1881.

CONTENTS.

TRUSTEES.

EXECUTORS AND ADMINISTRATORS.

INTRODUCTION.

This little book, intended to be essentially *practical* in its nature, is designed to be placed by lawyers in the hands of those of their clients who occupy the office of a trustee, whether as executor, administrator, assignee for the benefit of creditors, receiver, guardian, or committee of a lunatic, etc., or a trustee generally. It is not considered by the author to be a complete statement of all the duties of a trustee—by trustee we refer generally to any of the officers just mentioned—nor does it trace the course of all his proceedings, but it is simply intended to, and if regarded, *will*, we modestly believe, greatly aid the trustee in the administration of his trust, and save him and his counsel much time and annoyance, and the client under some circumstances personal liability and expense, by tending to put him upon inquiry as to his liabilities before taking some important step in the course of his proceedings, besides facilitating proceedings for his discharge, and the cancellation of his official bond, on winding up the trust estate. It is not its purpose to describe the attorney's duties, but only such as relate to the trustee himself. We do not wish to be understood as desiring that it shall in the least degree take the place of an attorney. There are no forms annexed. It is not intended that an executor should draw a petition to advertise for claims himself, but that he should know when his counsel may do it, and that until he has advertised he should not pay any debts or legacies where there is reason to believe that there will be a deficiency of assets. We are opposed to any system which purports to make "Every man his own lawyer for one dollar;" on the contrary, we advise every trustee at the outset to retain competent counsel. See third paragraph of Section 1 *post*. That "a little knowledge is a dangerous thing" is an aphorism peculiarly applicable to a knowledge of law and legal procedure, we fully realize; but every attorney, counsel for a trustee, well knows that there are many matters about which he desires to make suggestions to his client which escape his memory at the time, and although he answers all inquiries made of him, and spontaneously gives much information unasked, nevertheless there are many important subjects left undiscussed. We recently saw the report of a referee on an accounting, upon which a trustee was ordered by the Court in the decree to pay several hundred dollars interest from his own pocket, simply because he deposited the proceeds of the trust estate in his bank, in his own name, *individually*, and not "*as trustee*" (in whatever capacity). He doubtless stated to his counsel, and truly too, that he received no pecuniary benefit whatever from such deposit, and he probably asked why he was not told the proper way to deposit it, and thereby have been saved the money. The counsel either supposed that his client would know without being told, or, more likely, had forgotten to include that important item of information in the hundred and odd questions (some of them no doubt very trivial) he had answered. It is our desire to give the trustee in the following pages information of a similar character, with a view to relieving the attorney from taxing his memory with so many details of a like nature.

It is this responsibility for his many acts, committed and omitted, which makes the trustee a peculiar client, distinct from all others, *sui generis*. An ordinary plaintiff or defendant has generally but three duties to perform: *First*, to promptly pay all counsel fees called for; *second*, to keep his mouth shut about his case; and, *third*, to produce his witnesses on the trial; his counsel attends to everything else. But a trustee's personal duties are many and often perplexing; with every act scrutinized by from ten to three hundred parties in interest—oftener construed by such parties against him than in his favor—it is probably no exaggeration to say that fully seventy-five per cent of the trustees of estates of less than $25,000 in amount refuse to act in that capacity the second time.

The peculiar circumstances surrounding each case make it impossible in any book, large or small, to answer *all* practical questions that may arise; for those unanswered, and there are many, the trustee must consult his counsel.

Many trustees have an erroneous idea that immediately upon

assuming the duties of their office they become possessed for the time being of the trust estate, to deal with it as if it were their own property; forgetting that they must not only "Be as careful of other people's property as of their own," but *more* careful of it. There is a routine and detail which is irksome to some; they try to avoid it by saying, "Oh, I'm not so particular in my own business, why should I be with this?" The answer is, because he is a trustee.

It is barely possible that some attorneys may raise the objection that there is considerable information here given for which an attorney might make a charge to his client, a trustee, under the general head of "Consulting and advising."

To such objection we answer: "Nothing succeeds like success." As counsel for a trustee, it is, or ought to be, his sole object to have his client perform his duties with as little annoyance to the client as possible, to have him make no mistakes, avoid all difficulties, and finally receive his commission and obtain his discharge without being personally charged with a dollar. Such a result is always satisfactory alike to client and counsel. In such a case his own fees (it is presumed that the counsel for a trustee always takes a perspective view of his fees) would be equally as large as they would be if his client were charged with interest for using the funds of the estate, unintentionally probably, for his own benefit; or if he were obliged to defend him on the accounting for having sold the bulk of the trust property at private sale to his friends for small prices.

It is no *dis*advantage to counsel, for a trustee to obtain a certain amount of information as to his rights and duties from a source other than his counsel. We were recently informed of a case where a large law firm, composed of more than four prominent lawyers, acting under a conscientious misapprehension as to the rate at which their client's commissions as a trustee were to be computed, informed him at the time of his accounting that he was entitled to a certain amount at a certain rate. During the accounting it was discovered by a third party that they were properly to be computed at a rate which would produce *five* times the amount supposed by the counsel, and in the decree the trustee was allowed such larger amount by the Court. The Courts always *assume* that such general instruction and advice as is contained in the following pages, is given, and they act on that assumption when they charge a trustee for any loss to the estate resulting from his improper acts.

It is expected that counsel will elaborate upon matters merely suggested here.

The counsel for the successful trustee is generally well paid for his services, and he ought to be, for he is engaged in one of the most laborious branches of the profession.

That "Time is money" is a maxim as much appreciated by the lawyer in active practice as by any business man.

The counsel for twenty-five trustees would, if he had the time, like to have fifty for clients. Surely anything which *tends*, in however small a degree, to assist him to acquire such increase, is not inimical to his interests.

If the trustee does not here find *everything* necessary for him to know to make his task easy, he will, at least, be led by a perusal of these pages to do what many trustees fail to do, and by their omission get into trouble—that is, to ask their counsel for information upon subjects here simply suggested, before proceeding in any important matter connected with their trusts.

We have endeavored, the book being intended for laymen, to use very plain language, and trust that the reason for it will be seen without being stated here. R. P. L.

No. 4 Warren Street, New York,
June 23, 1881.

TRUSTEES.

SECTION 1.—*Under this general head of "Trustees" we include suggestions relating generally to executors, administrators, assignees, receivers, guardians, and other trustees; for they are all "trustees," though there is a technical difference which we do not deem it necessary here to discuss; and the attention of each of those officers is directed to the remarks under this title, as they concern them equally as much as if they were included under their respective titles, where information more exclusively for them is to be found.*

A trustee is "a person in whom some estate, interest, or power in or affecting property of any description, is vested for the benefit of another." Generally, any person of full age and sound mind may be a trustee.

A trustee of any kind ought never to attempt to perform any of the duties which are properly a lawyer's, all petitions, orders, applications to the court of any nature, receipts, vouchers, contracts, notices, advertisements, etc., should always be prepared by his counsel, so also should all schedules, inventories, and accounts, the trustee furnishing his counsel with full memoranda as hereinafter referred to, to enable the counsel to prepare such papers, inventories, and accounts; where a trustee being a layman attempts to perform an attorney's duties he almost invariably gets into trouble, he is never allowed any extra compensation because he performed any part of a lawyer's duties in addition to his own, and courts always allow a reasonable compensation to be paid by the trustee to his counsel, no matter how small the estate is.

Where the words "former party" are used in these pages, they refer: in proceedings in the Surrogate's Court, to the "decedent," or deceased person; in assignment proceedings, to the assignor; in trusteeships generally, to the person who, prior to the trustee's entry upon his administration, owned the trust property and estate.

A trustee, though occupying a prominent place in the business community, with an established reputation for honor and integrity, immediately upon accepting the management of a trust estate places himself in a position where he is open to criticism; disappointed people, who do not receive upon the death of a relative as large a portion of his estate as they expected, and creditors, upon the failure of a debtor, who are not preferred in an assignment, angered and chagrined because they have not the power to alter the will or assignment, always imagine that they punish the "former party" for neglecting them by annoying the trustee in the management of his estate—in effect, they say to the trustee, "We believe that you are dishonest, that you desire to use your position for your own benefit; show us by your acts and by your accounting that you have administered the estate for the interest of the beneficiaries, or parties entitled to share in the estate or its proceeds;" but if his proceedings are *straight* and regular, he need not have the *slightest* fear, as all courts are very favorably disposed toward trustees who exhibit a willingness to properly perform their duties.

SECTION 2. Books of Account.—A little care on the part of a trustee to keep a complete record of all his proceedings will save him much trouble. If he cannot spare the time to make memoranda and entries of his proceedings and accounts himself in his books, including brief mention of any important event—so that on his accounting he may not only remember that the transaction occurred, but also the *particulars* of it—he should employ some one to do it for him, under his direction, at stated intervals, say once or twice a week, or every day if necessary. If the payment for this service is reasonable it would probably be allowed out of the estate. He should, immediately on entering upon his duties, provide himself with proper books of account (*proper* books should show the details of all his transactions), in which entries should be made *at the time* of all moneys received and paid out on account of the estate—full particulars and items of any considerable amount should be given. In regard to receipts and payments it should clearly appear: 1. *When*, the year, month, and day, the money was received or paid out. 2. *From whom* it was received, or *to whom* it was paid—giving the person's *full* name and address. 3. *For what purpose* or *upon whose account* it was received or paid out, giving full particulars. (For instance, it is insufficient to state simply "Expenses," or "Expenses for business," or, if he should go to Boston, it is not enough to state, "Expenses to Boston, $50; he should state *who* went to Boston, and *what for*, giving the items.) 4. The *exact amount* which was received or paid out. All these facts must be shown on the accounting, and it is *much* easier to make a memorandum of them at the time than to attempt to remember them months and perhaps years afterward. Take three or four lines to each item, if necessary. 5. If a payment of any considerable amount was made, an entry should be made of the number of the voucher for it. *All entries in his books should be made chronologically*—that is, in the exact order of the time of the occurrence of the transactions—and they should so appear in his account.

SECTION 3. Schedules and Inventory.—The attention of all trustees is directed to Section 41, "Schedules and Inventory," under the head of "Assignees," as the remarks in that section relate in many respects to all trustees. A trustee should carefully examine the schedule and inventory to see that the values of the stock, property, and outstanding debts are therein correctly given, the actual values should not be excessive, remembering creditors' and beneficiaries' rights. He should see, if possible, that all the property mentioned in the inventory is or was actually in the former party's possession, or that he is entitled to the possession of it, or claims to be entitled to the possession of it. The attention of assignees is particularly called to this section, for the schedules and inventory are taken as *presumptive* though not conclusive evidence of all property which came into his hands (and when they are filed by the trustee himself they are in the nature of an admission to that effect), and at the *values* therein stated; and he will be held accountable for all property therein mentioned. The inventory is the basis upon which his accounting proceeds, and he will be charged with the property and at the values there mentioned, unless he can show that he did not receive such property, or that such values were excessive; he should therefore see that the actual values as stated in the inventory are not too high, and in determining such value he should consider the prices he will obtain upon a sale under the circumstances. If in preparing or assisting to prepare the inventory (and an inventory *always should* be prepared and filed at the commencement of the proceedings), he is unable to arrive at the values because of his being unfamiliar with the nature of the property or the "former party's" business; then he should obtain the services of a person who is, to the end that a fair valuation may appear. If the property should realize *more* than the values stated in the inventory, any *increase* belongs to the estate; whereas he is accountable for, and must explain, any *decrease. A trustee cannot in any manner use or employ the trust estate or its proceeds for his own profit.* An account should be kept, and an entry made in his books as an "important event," of any property which may come into his hands not included in the schedules or inventory; he must account for this just as though it were set out in the inventory, as originally filed.

A copy of the schedules and inventory in assignment matters, and the inventory in Surrogate's and other proceedings, should be obtained by the trustee at the commencement of his administration for his guidance; so that he may always see for what property he must account, what outstanding debts, etc., he must collect, and he must remember that he will be closely questioned on his accounting as to what disposition he made of the property, and he will be expected to show that he realized the values named therein, or, if he did not, he must show *why* he did not.

When the sheriff makes a levy, under writs from the courts, upon any portion of the estate, the trustee should *always* make and keep a careful inventory or statement of all the property so taken, and should measure and ascertain the exact quantity of the goods and property taken (if it is of a nature incapable of measurement, it should be described so as to be readily identified), and have the sheriff to give a receipt.

Whenever the trustee is served with any legal papers, he should *immediately* make a memorandum on them of day, month, and year when served upon him, and send them to his counsel at once.

SECTION 4. Bank Account.—A trustee should always keep a bank account of moneys belonging to the trust estate, or an account of any kind relating to the trust property, entirely separate from his own individual account, or his firm's account. It should stand in his name as trustee, thus: "——— Bank, in account with ——— ——— as (executor or assignee) of the estate of ———." *He should always keep the trust property in any form, and its proceeds, entirely separate and distinct from his own; a failure to do this will not only render him and his sureties liable for any loss occasioned thereby, but will also result in his being charged with interest, and in some cases with compound interest, to be paid from his own funds.* Any trustee who now has trust funds of the estate deposited in his own name should immediately transfer the account as above.

SECTION 5. Interest.—*He will be charged with interest if he mingles the trust funds with his own*, although he made no profit thereby; he will be compelled to pay interest if he in any way employs the funds for his own advantage; but in general he will not be charged with interest where he holds funds from which he is obliged to make frequent payments; but if he retain moneys for any considerable length of time he may be charged with interest. He is allowed six months generally to invest the funds, but it is safer for him to *deposit* the funds where they will draw interest if possible.

SECTION 6. Rent.—The trustee should always enter into a new contract with the landlord of the premises occupied by him for the period during which he actually occupies them. He should be careful not to give any preference to the landlord, nor to assume any of the "former party's" contracts with him. Of course he should not engage himself to pay a large rent for the purposes of winding up the estate, unless it is clearly apparent that it will be of benefit to the estate for him to do so.

SECTION 7. Sales.—In the majority of cases, in the absence of specific directions in the instrument under which he acts, it is safer and better for the trustee, *immediately* after taking possession of the trust estate, lawfully, to sell it at *auction*, and *not* at private sale. He is protected by an auction sale, fairly conducted and had upon *proper* notice (he should always consult his counsel as to the length of notice and the manner in which it should be given), even though the prices obtained are much lower than he could get at private sale. An AUCTION *sale*, honestly conducted, had upon proper notice and after due publicity, *cannot be impeached*, and the trustee cannot be successfully attacked because the prices obtained were inadequate ; but upon a private sale under certain circumstances he can be made liable for any deficiency between the prices obtained and those which opposing parties may make it appear to the Court *ought* to have been obtained. He should always give notice of the sale (at auction or not) to the beneficiaries or persons entitled to share in the estate ; by doing this he gives them the *opportunity* which they *may* avail themselves of—that is, of purchasing at fifty per cent higher prices than any other parties attending the sale would give. He should never sell at retail, as a rule, unless he is directed to do so by the instrument under which he acts (an assignee never should). There are a *very* few instances where he will be justified in selling at private sale, but when he does he should be very careful to sell for what he *knows* to be good prices, and *higher* than he could get at auction. He will be compelled to sustain his action on his accounting, and show that the manner of sale was for the benefit of the estate.

As it is sometimes necessary to obtain the order of the Court to authorize a sale, he should never sell any property until he has first made that inquiry of counsel. Upon the sale of real property he should be careful to observe all legal formalities, with two objects in view—first, to give a good title to the purchaser by having all proceedings regular, and, second, for his own protection. In these sales also he should be careful to sell, or to attempt to sell rather, his "right, title, and interest" in the property to be sold, and to avoid all warranties or guaranties. He may sell what he received from his grantor ; he cannot give a better title than he received, and should not attempt it. In releases, however, although he may release or quit claim a piece of land, he really releases only his actual interest in it.

He should never sell property at private sale without knowing its value, and if he is personally unacquainted with it, he should have it appraised by competent appraisers. Property should *generally* be sold in its primary state, or as the trustee finds it, and he should not spend money or purchase other material to manufacture it into the articles intended by the "former party"; if he does he must be prepared on his accounting to show that such action resulted in a pecuniary benefit to the estate—sometimes a difficult matter to establish.

SECTION 8. Advertising.—The trustee should always give as much publicity and notoriety to his sales of property as possible—the more the better; it has a tendency to bring together a large number of would-be buyers, and increases the proceeds of the sale thereby, and shows that the trustee is perfectly willing that his proceedings in relation to the sale shall be examined, that he has no secret interests to guard. He should always advertise the sale of both real and personal property in at least two newspapers. In some classes of trustees the requisite number of times that the notice of sale should be advertised is regulated by rule or statute; but in most instances it is a matter of discretion with the trustee. He should advertise all sales at least once a week for three weeks successively, and particularly real estate, which, if valuable, should be advertised once a week for six successive weeks prior to the date of sale. The trustee should be careful to preserve his receipts or vouchers obtained from the newspapers upon payment of their charges for advertising, however small in amount, as the Court requires *proof* of the due advertisement of all notices, and this proof is furnished by the affidavit of the publisher, principal clerk, or foreman of the newspaper, identifying the notice and the number of times, and when it was inserted. The newspapers generally require the production of their receipts before delivering the affidavit mentioned, so that they may know that the party paying for the advertisement is the one who received the proof. These affidavits should *always* be procured by the trustee *immediately* after the last insertion of the advertisement in the newspaper. It is very difficult, and perhaps impossible, for the newspaper to supply it after the lapse of a long delay after the completion of the advertisement. The proofs or affidavits should be carefully preserved by the trustee, to be used on his accounting. Most newspapers will furnish "slips," or extra copies of the advertisement or notice for a trivial sum above the charge for advertising.

There are some newspapers designated by law and the rules of the courts in which all legal notices must be advertised. Where creditors, claimants, or any parties in interest reside without the State of New York, all notices intended for *them* must be advertised in the "State paper," published at Albany. At present the "State paper" is *The Albany Morning Express;*" office, corner Green and Beaver Streets, Albany, New York. It will continue to be the State paper until March 8th, 1885. In each county there is a newspaper in which legal advertisements should be inserted. In the county of New York *The Daily Register*, office, No. 303 Broadway, is the official law journal of the county, and all advertised notices of proceedings of any nature, in cases in the courts of that county, should always be inserted in that journal. All newspapers require that legal advertisements shall be paid for in advance.

SECTION 9. Names of Purchasers.—The trustee should always ascertain and enter in his books the full names and addresses of parties who purchase property composing the trust estate from him, either at auction or private sale, with quantities purchased,and the amounts paid therefore. He should also keep a memorandum of *when* the sale occurred. It has a prejudicial appearance for him not to know to whom he sells the property forming the trust estate. He should always retain a copy of the catalogue of an auction sale, with the prices obtained for *each lot* marked thereon, to be used on his accounting; he should also retain a copy of any posters or hand-bills advertising the sale for the same purpose.

A trustee himself *cannot* properly *be a purchaser of any of the trust property*, nor can he have any one purchase it for him, or in his behalf, either at auction or private sale; if he does, the sale may be set aside. It is a general principle of the law governing trustees, that a trustee cannot place himself in a position antagonistic to his trust, or against its best interests; and he would be doing so were he to become a purchaser on the sale of the trust property, because in that event he would naturally desire that it should sell for as *little* as possible, whereas, properly, he should desire and exert himself to have it sell for as *much* as possible.

SECTION 10. Credit.—In general he should not give any credit or time whatever upon the sale of any of the trust property (an assignee or executor *never* should) ; if he does it is at his own personal risk, and he should remember that when he incurs a personal risk he also renders his sureties liable.

SECTION 11. Statement of Moneys Received for Outstanding Debts Collected, and from Sales, should be separate.—The amounts received for stock and property sold, either at auction or private sale, should *always* be kept entirely *separate* and distinct from the statement of amounts received on account of outstanding debts due the estate which the trustee has collected ; and under no circumstances should they all be included in one *item*. The attention of assignees is particularly called to this section.

SECTION 12. Vouchers.—Vouchers, commonly called receipts, should always be taken by a trustee, and carefully preserved by him, upon payment of all sums amounting to five dollars or over. (Of course this amount is arbitrary ; he *can* demand a receipt for a payment of *ten cents,* and he is not absolutely compelled to take one for $19.50, but it is decidedly the better way to take vouchers down to at least $5 ; in large estates this amount may be too small and produce too many vouchers ; in such case a larger sum can be fixed upon, not exceeding $20 ; it reminds him of the transaction, and the exact cause of the disbursement, and it relieves him of a great deal of swearing.) The law *absolutely requires that vouchers shall be produced* on the trustee's accounting for all payments exceeding twenty dollars ($20), and that he must swear POSITIVELY that he actually made for the benefit of the estate all payments amounting to less than that sum, giving full particulars as to *exact amounts,* to *whom paid,* and *the object of the payment,* and that the total of such payments unsupported by vouchers shall not exceed $500, on all accountings, by all trustees, in any one case.

☞ *Any payment over twenty dollars* ($20) *for which no voucher is produced will be disallowed, and when a payment is disallowed, the trustee must lose the amount of such payment from his own pocket.* When the trustee pays money to himself he should always give a receipt or voucher to himself "as trustee" (assignor or executor, for instance) in the same form as from other persons; this is not always conclusive as to the fact of payment.

A voucher should be numbered so as to correspond in number with the payment to which it relates, which should also be numbered, so as to distinguish them, as payments of the same *amount* and for the same *object* are frequently made at different *times*. For example, in the statement of payments by the trustee, suppose the first item to be as follows: "1881, July 1. John Jacob Astor, 85 Prince Street, New York, for rent of premises No. 500 Broadway, New York, occupied by assignee for month of June, 1881, $250." On the left margin of the book this item should be numbered "No. 1" with colored pencil or ink (and the voucher should be marked "No. 1" to correspond).

All vouchers for payments by, and all bills rendered to, the trustee after he enters upon the discharge of his duties for any indebtedness incurred by *him* since his appointment, *must* be in the name of the *trustee*, "as trustee (executor, assignee, etc.) of the estate of ———;" that is, the bills and claims represented thereby should be against the *trustee*, and not against the "former party;" it must appear *by the bill or voucher* that the *trustee* incurred the debt and paid the money. Where a trustee now holds bills or vouchers for any indebtedness incurred by *him* since his appointment, and which bills were rendered to him, but in the "former party's" name, he should immediately obtain from the party rendering the bill a new bill or voucher by which it should appear that the claim was against *the trustee* (and it should mention his name, and not the "former party's," as aforesaid). The attention of assignees is *particularly* called to this suggestion, as a failure to observe it will result in their defective vouchers being thrown out, and the payment disallowed.

A correct voucher should show the following facts: 1. The exact date *when* the money was paid, day, month, and year. 2. From *whom* it was received, and *in what capacity* of the party making the payment—"as executor, etc., of ———, deceased," for instance. 3. The exact *amount* paid. 4. The *object* of payment, stated briefly as "my salary for one week as porter" (always giving full particulars, so that it will be unnecessary for his counsel in making up his accounts on his accounting to ask a dozen questions in regard to each item); and 5. The legible signature of the party to whom the payment was made, by himself personally, or by his duly authorized agent for him, in which case the agent should sign the principal's name, and afterward his own name after the word "by;" but as a rule the agent should not sign except in the absence of his principal. More care should be taken in this respect because of the trust relation than in case of individuals perhaps.

Vouchers should be on paper about the size of legal cap or letter paper, the larger the better, and less the liability that they will be mislaid or lost; paper is cheap, and every court will allow the trustee to buy enough for vouchers of proper size. Some trustees have an erroneous idea that it is an indication of economy in their administration, for them to take a receipt for a payment of $1000 on a scrap of paper about the size of a postage stamp.

It is advantageous to have the vouchers *printed* on legal cap (or paper about that size), and bound in book form, with the court and title of the proceedings, thus:

Surrogate's Court, New York County.

In the Matter of the Estate of Christopher Columbus, deceased.

NEW YORK, , 188 .

Received from William H. Prescott and James Russell Lowell, executors, etc., of Christopher Columbus, deceased, the sum of dollars.

(Here leave ample space in which to insert the object of payment.)

The word "No." should be printed at *bottom* left-hand corner. Vouchers similar to this may always be identified at a glance; they are all of uniform size; they are in a neat and compact form, are well preserved, easy to refer to, and easy to bind together when the proceedings are ended.

Care should be taken to have the vouchers contain no memoranda of a personal character which the trustee might desire to keep, as the vouchers at the close of the accounting must be filed in court permanently.

SECTION 13. Outstanding Debts and Claims.—The trustee should make *diligent* efforts to collect *all* outstanding debts and claims due the estate, and properly he should not call in the services of a collecting agency until he has ascertained that he is unable to collect them without such assistance. On his accounting he will be rigidly questioned in regard to *each claim* due the estate, and if any are uncollected, he will be asked *why* he did not collect them. He must also then be prepared to show the cause for any difference between the amounts stated in the schedules or inventory in the list of outstandings and the amounts of such outstandings shown by his account to have been collected. He should make an entry in his books at the time of payment of the reasons for the difference (whether of discounts, offsets, goods returned, etc., giving the particulars), so that they may appear in his final account—that is, the difference between the face of the claim as given in the inventory and the amount actually collected.

SECTION 14. Compromising Claims due the Estate.—A trustee has the right generally to compromise or compound a claim due the estate; but, as in some cases it should be done only upon the order of the Court upon notice to all beneficiaries and parties in interest, he should never compromise a claim without first consulting his counsel. Generally he will have to show on his accounting that the amount received in compromise was the largest possible to be obtained.

SECTION 15. Insurance, Taxes, etc.—He may properly pay necessary insurance premiums, taxes, etc.; but he should be careful to ascertain so as to be able to show that such disbursements were for the benefit of the estate.

SECTION 16. Proofs of Debt or Claims against the Estate.—These should be *carefully preserved.* The trustee should endorse upon the proof the name of the court in which the proceeding is pending and the title of the case (so that any one viewing it from the outside will not throw it away as waste paper), together with the day, month, and year when it was filed with him, as follows: "Court, title of case, proof of claim of John Brown, 400 Broadway, N. Y., $1200. Filed with trustee (assignee or executor) April 20th, 1881;" adding his initials. He should also obtain from the party filing it the *address* of the claimant or creditor, street and number, which should also be endorsed on the proof, with the amount of the claim. He should also enter in his *books* the full name of the creditor or claimant, his address, the amount of his claim, and date of filing with him. The object of this is to keep a record of claimants' names and addresses, amounts, etc., so that in the event of the proof itself being lost his books will show who filed it, etc. The preservation of these claims is important, as generally only such claimants as thus prove their claims are entitled to share in the proceeds of the estate.

If a proof of claim is once filed with a trustee, he should not allow the party filing it, or any one else, to take it from him again for any reason. If the party filing has omitted something or made a mistake of any kind, inform him that he may file an *amended* proof if he desires to do so, but retain the old one.

SECTION 17. Dividend.—The trustee should always figure the amount of any dividend due to creditors or other beneficiaries himself, or have his clerk do it. It is not his counsel's place to do it; the trustee having the funds in his custody, it is better that he should calculate the payments to be made himself. He should always take a receipt or voucher from a party to whom a dividend is paid; the voucher should be entitled in the proceedings, and should be written or printed to correspond with each other, and should be acknowledged before a notary public or officer of similar powers, the fees for which are payable out of the estate. He should give notice to all parties in interest of the payment of a dividend, and if a meeting is held for the purpose of computing its amount, of the time and place of the meeting, and in some cases of notice to present claims before that time.

SECTION 18. Accounting.—A trustee should always account as soon as he can ; and *generally* speaking he *can* when the object of creating the trust has been realized, carried out, or accomplished. The lapse of time is frequently the cause of annoyance, additional expense, and delay in the proceedings, and in some cases the trustee may be charged personally with the cost of proceedings taken to compel him to account. On his accounting he must show generally what disposition he has made with the trust property and estate ; how he has performed his duties ; what property has come into his hands, as appears by the inventory filed at the commencement of the proceedings ; how much of that has actually come into his hands ; why all of it has not come into his possession, showing any depreciation in values, discounts, goods returned, amounts, etc. ; why he did not collect *all* outstanding debts due the estate ; the exact amounts of such as he *did* collect ; why he actually received less than the face amount of the claim ; how he sold the property, whether by auction or at private sale, the exact amounts received therefor ; the exact amounts of all payments, showing the date of payment, to whom, for what purpose, vouchers, etc.; and, lastly, the balance remaining in his hands at the date of filing his account.

His whole proceedings and all his acts (particularly such as are in these pages referred to) in the care and management of the estate come up for review on his accounting.

SECTION 19. Reserved Fund.—A trustee, before making any payments for expenses, claims of creditors, dividends, etc., should always retain in his hands a "reserve fund"—that is, a certain sum of money to meet contingent expenses, as on the final settlement of the estate it frequently occurs that unforeseen payments have to be made. The amount of this fund must vary in different cases. It should cover before everything of course, the trustee's commissions ; next, the expenses of his accounting, including referee's fees, advertising, etc., and allowances to counsel. We have seen several cases where trustees had to *personally* bear the expenses of their accounting because of their failure to retain the funds of the estate necessary for that purpose ; but he must exercise an honest discretion of course in fixing upon the amount he ought to retain ; $100,000, for instance, would ordinarily be too large—too much like a "sinking fund." Of course this "reserve fund" being a *part* generally of the estate, must be entirely used up or distributed by proper payments before the trustee is finally discharged.

SECTION 20. Resignation—Removal.—If a trustee accepts his appointment and enters upon the discharge of his duties, he cannot relinquish the trust entirely of his own motion. To resign and be properly discharged, he should through his counsel petition the Court, account for all funds and property which have come into his hands, and then, after notice to all parties interested, he can be duly discharged by an order of the Court having jurisdiction. He should show some reason for desiring to resign. Misconduct and insolvency generally are causes for a trustee's removal. Of course the misconduct must be some material impropriety, such as a refusal to perform his duties, or where he is guilty of fraud, etc.

EXECUTORS AND ADMINISTRATORS.

☞ *The attention of executors and administrators is directed to all information and instructions under the head of "Trustees," as the matter there to be found is just as important to executors and administrators as that contained under this title (which relates more exclusively to them), and is not repeated here simply to avoid repetition.*

The provisions of law governing executors and administrators are almost identical.

SECTION 21. Who may be an Executor.—Any person may be an executor or executrix in this State who is of sound mind, over twenty-one years of age, capable of making a contract, and who is not an alien—that is, a resident of a foreign *country* (a resident of another *State* of the United States may be an executor in this State)—and who has not been convicted of an infamous crime (by "infamous crime," as used in the statute, is meant every offence punishable with death, or by imprisonment in a State prison, and no other). No one can be an executor who on proper proof shall be deemed by the Surrogate to be incompetent by reason of drunkenness, dishonesty, improvidence, or want of understanding; and it is discretionary with the Surrogate to appoint as executor or administrator one who cannot read and write the English language. Formerly a married woman could not act as executrix without her husband's consent; but like many other barbarous restrictions against gentle woman all disabilities have been removed, and she may now act as executrix, administratrix, guardian, etc., in the same manner as if she were sole or unmarried.

SECTION 22. Who is Entitled to be an Administrator.—The same legal requirements exist as to the right of a person to be an administrator as to an executor as above set forth. A testator (a testator is a person who makes a will) may appoint any competent person his executor or executrix, but the law requires the *Surrogate* to appoint a legally competent person an administrator or administratrix, in the following order of preference: *First.* To the widow (or husband). *Second.* To the children. *Third.* To the father. *Fourth.* To the mother. *Fifth.* To the brothers. *Sixth.* To the sisters. *Seventh.* To the grandchildren. *Eighth.* To any of the next of kin who would be entitled to share in the distribution of the estate. If any persons entitled are minors (that is, under the age of 21 years), administration shall be granted to their guardians. If none of the relatives of the deceased will accept the appointment, then the creditors of the deceased will be appointed; the one applying first will be entitled to a preference; but in New York and Kings counties the Public Administrator has a preference after the relatives and before creditors and all other persons. Where there are several persons of the same degree of relationship to the intestate (an intestate is one who dies without leaving a will) entitled to administration, they are preferred in the following order: *First.* Males to females. *Second.* Relatives of the whole blood to those of the half blood. *Third.* Unmarried women to such as are married. And where there are several persons equally entitled, the Surrogate may in his discretion grant letters of administration to one or more of such persons.

Where all the executors named in a will do not for any reason enter upon the discharge of their duties, the Surrogate appoints a residuary legatee, or any other legatee, and if they decline then the next of kin are appointed according to the foregoing order of preference, an administrator with the will annexed, who stands in all respects in the position of an executor.

SECTION 23. Renunciation or Acceptance of Appointment.—No one can be compelled to accept his appointment as executor or administrator, but an executor must renounce his appointment in a formal manner, or fail to qualify after due notice to do so, before the Surrogate will appoint some other person. He may withdraw his renunciation at any time before letters are actually issued, but having once accepted he cannot renounce. The renunciation must be in writing, attested by two witnesses, acknowledged or proved before a notary or similar officer, and filed with the Surrogate.

If a person named as executor fails to appear before the Surrogate and take the oath of office within thirty days after the will is proved, not having renounced meanwhile, a summons will be issued by the Surrogate requiring him to appear and qualify, and if he fails to do so within the time named in the summons he will be deemed to have renounced.

In case of the death of one of several executors, or if for any reason one or more shall cease to act, the survivor or survivors proceed to complete the administration of the estate alone, in the same manner as if the deceased or retiring executor had never been named in the will. Executors and administrators hold their estate as "joint tenants," and are considered in law as one person, and they are presumed to act together in all that they do.

SECTION 24. Bond—Security.—An executor is not obliged to give a bond if he reside in this State, unless he is ordered to do so by the Surrogate, and the Surrogate will not make such an order unless the will directs that the executor shall give a bond, or where objection is made that the pecuniary circumstances of the executor are such that they do not afford adequate security to the parties interested in the estate, or because he is not a resident of this State; but a non-resident executor will not be required to give a bond if he has an office within the State for the regular transaction of business in person, and the will contains an express provision to the effect that he may act without giving security. When a bond is required of an executor, it is to the same effect, amount, etc., as an administrator's bond. But an executor will not be required to give security simply because he is not as rich a man as the testator was, or anywhere approaching it; it is necessary simply that he should be *responsible* in the general acceptation of that word.

An administrator must *always* give a bond, the amount of which is fixed by the Surrogate pursuant to statute, and the following is a copy of Section 2267 of the Code of Civil Procedure, and is now the law relating thereto.

" Section 2667. A person appointed an administrator must, before letters are issued to him, besides filing his official oath, execute to the people of the State, and file with the Surrogate, the joint and several bond of himself and two or more sureties, in a penalty fixed by the Surrogate, not less than twice the value of the personal property of which the decedent died possessed, and of the probable amount to be recovered by reason of any right of action, granted to an executor or administrator by special provision of law. The sum to be fixed as the amount of the penalty must be ascertained by the Surrogate, by the examination upon oath, of the applicant or any other person, or otherwise, as the Surrogate thinks proper. The bond must be conditioned that the administrator will faithfully discharge the trust reposed in him as such, and obey all lawful decrees and orders of the Surrogate's court, touching the administration of the estate committed to him."

By an amendment of 1881, Section 2667 is so amended as to permit the Surrogate to accept modified security from an executor or administrator and issue limited letters where a right of action is given to him by special provision of law; as to sue for damages for causing the decedent's death, etc.

If there is more than one administrator, one bond executed by all will answer, with sureties of course.

Any person interested in the estate may require sureties to justify before the Surrogate or his chief clerk, and submit to an examination as to their sufficiency, upon at least five days' notice to the executor or administrator. If the sureties are deemed sufficient the bond will be approved, if insufficient the Surrogate will make an order requiring substitution of new sureties within five days after service of a copy of said order upon the executor, administrator or trustee, or his attorney.

It is the rule of the Surrogate of New York County to require that at least one of the sureties on an administrator's bond over $500 in amount, shall be a freeholder (or owner of real estate) within this State.

In large estates it is often a difficult matter for an executor or administrator to give a bond with sureties who are able or willing to justify in double the penalty of the bond, and among the good features of the new Code of Civil Procedure is Section

2595, which relieves an executor or administrator in such cases. It reads as follows:

"Section 2595. In a case where a bond, or new sureties to a bond, may be required by a Surrogate from an executor, administrator, or other trustee, if the value of the estate or fund is so great that the Surrogate deems it inexpedient to require security in the full amount prescribed by law, he may direct that any securities for the payment of money belonging to the estate or fund be deposited with him, to be delivered to the County Treasurer, or be deposited subject to the order of the trustee, countersigned by the Surrogate, with a trust company duly authorized by law to receive the same. After such a deposit has been made, the Surrogate may fix the amount of the bond with respect to the value of the remainder only of the estate or fund. A security thus deposited shall not be withdrawn from the custody of the County Treasurer or trust company, and no person, other than the County Treasurer or the proper officer of the trust company, shall receive or collect any of the principal or interest secured thereby, without the special order of the Surrogate, entered in the appropriate book. Such an order can be made in favor of the trustee appointed, only where an additional bond has been given by him, or upon proof that the estate or fund has been so reduced by payments or otherwise, that the penalty of the bond originally given will be sufficient in amount to satisfy the provisions of law relating to the penalty thereof, if the security so withdrawn is also reckoned in the estate or fund."

Pursuant to the foregoing section the Surrogate of the County of New York has established the following among other new rules relating to his court: "Rule XVII. The deposit of securities for the payment of money belonging to an estate or fund, as provided in Section 2595 of the Code of Procedure, for the purpose of reducing the bond of an executor, administrator, or other trustee, shall be made under the order of tho Surrogate, in the Union Trust Company of the city of New York, subject to the order of the trustee, to be countersigned by the Surrogate, and not otherwise."

Any party interested may show to the Surrogate that the bond is insufficient for any cause, and if the Surrogate orders a new bond or sureties they must be furnished within five days from the date of the order, or the letters will be revoked. Any or all of the sureties on a bond in the Surrogate's Court may present a petition to that court praying to be released from responsibility on account of any future breach of the condition of the bond, and the administrator must file a new bond with new sureties within five days after he is ordered to do so.

SECTION 25. Appraisal.—After the bond is given, where necessary, the next act on the part of the executor or administrator is to apply to the Surrogate for the appointment of two disinterested persons to act as appraisers, to estimate the value of the personal property. This they proceed to do with the aid of the executor or administrator, after due notice of the time and place of the appraisal has been given to all parties interested; and an inventory should be prepared for the use of the appraiser showing the property and assets in detail, and after the valuations are affixed to it by the appraiser it may be used and filed as the inventory proper. The executor or administrator should make it his business to attend the appraisal, and should see that a just valuation is put on the property, so that on his accounting he will be saved the trouble of showing that an excessive value was unintentionally given to certain property by the appraisers, and he may then be able to learn from conversation with legatees and others the nature of the property, its true value, etc., and other information that will be useful to him.

SECTION 26. Inventory.—This must be filed by the executor or administrator within a reasonable time, and *must* be filed within three months from the date of his letters. The inventory is a list or statement of all the property and assets composing the estate, with its appraised value. The inventory must be sworn to by the executor to the effect that it is in all respects just and true, and contains a true statement of all the personal property of the deceased which has come to his knowledge, and particularly of all money, bank bills, and other circulating medium, belonging to the deceased, and of all just claims of the deceased against such executor or administrator, according to the best of his knowledge. The statement should be full, giving all *details and particulars*, including any *incumbrances*, etc.

The Surrogate may order an executor or administrator who persists in his refusal to file an inventory, to be lodged in jail until he files it, or pays the funds in his hands to his successor. When property comes into the hands of the executor or administrator not included in the inventory, he must apply to have it appraised, and an inventory of it prepared within two months after he discovers it. Where the executor is tardy in filing the inventory, and he only does so when ordered by the Surrogate upon the application of a party in interest, he may be charged personally with the payment of the cost of the proceedings taken to compel him to file it. If only one of several executors or administrators file his inventory, those neglecting cannot interfere with or have any power over the personal estate, but the one who filed the inventory has the sole administration until the others make and file their inventory as require by law.

The inventory is *primâ facie* evidence of the value of the estate. Any increase over the values there stated belongs to the estate, and any decrease must be explained on the accounting.

SECTION 27. Articles set Apart by Statute for the Use of Decedent's Widow and Minor Children.—The statute declares that where a man having a family dies, certain articles shall be considered as exempt, and the executor or administrator has no control over these except to take possession of them simply for the purpose of including them in the inventory, without being appraised. He holds such property in trust, not for the benefit of creditors or legatees, but for the decedent's widow and minor children, and they *cannot be disposed of* by the testator by his will; but they remain in possession of the widow, if there be one, during the time she shall live with and provide for the minor child or children. If there be a widow and no minor child, then such articles belong to the widow. When the children, if any, come of age, she is entitled to such property absolutely. Where a widow dies leaving a minor child or children, the same articles are to be set apart for the minors as are set apart for the widow in the case of a man dying.

The following are the articles enumerated by the statute:

"1. All spinning wheels, weaving looms, one knitting machine, one sewing machine, and stoves put up or kept for use, by his family.

"2. The family Bible, family pictures, and school books used by or in the family of such deceased person, and books not exceeding in value fifty dollars, which were kept and used as part of the family library before the decease of such person.

"3. All sheep to the number of ten, with their fleeces, and the yarn and cloth manufactured from the same; one cow (it must be a milch cow, if there is one in the estate); two swine, and the pork of such swine, and the necessary food for such swine, sheep or cow for sixty days, and all necessary provisions and fuel for such widow or child or children for sixty days after the death of such deceased person.

"4. All necessary wearing apparel, beds, bedsteads, and bedding; necessary cooking utensils, the clothing of the family, the clothes of the widow and her ornaments proper for her station; one table, six chairs, twelve knives and forks, twelve plates, twelve tea-cups and saucers, one sugar dish, one milk-pot, one tea-pot, and twelve spoons, and also other household furniture which shall not exceed one hundred and fifty dollars in value."

SECTION 28. Power over Estate.—An executor or administrator has no power to dispose of the estate until after letters are granted to him, except to preserve it and to pay funeral charges; though in law he is considered as taking possession at the instant after the testator's death, so that his power after he has qualified relates back to the decedent's death. An executor should supply himself with a true copy of the *will* as soon as he enters upon his duties, and he should always carefully follow its directions in his administration, but he should not attempt to act upon his own interpretation of any abstruse provision of it.

SECTION 29. Taking Possession.—He should take possession of the estate after the return of the inventory. He may obtain the process of the court to assist him in case any person refuses to deliver the property. He should take possession of all papers, etc., relating to the personal estate. For the purpose of taking possession he has all the powers of the decedent over the property. He holds the property, however, as trustee for the legatees or next of kin. Two or more executors or administrators are considered as one person; the entire estate is held by them jointly. Upon the death of one the title to the estate vests in the survivors, until they all die or are removed.

The law requires that where the will relates to real property, the executor, or administrator, with the will annexed, must cause the same to be recorded, with the certificate of proof annexed thereto, or endorsed thereon, in each county where real property of the testator is situated, within twenty days after letters are issued to him; but, by an amendment of 1881, a copy duly exemplified by the Surrogate will be accepted for record by a County Clerk or Register in place of the original will.

Employment of Agent.—Where the executor or administrator can show that his employment of an agent benefited the estate, or he is authorized to employ one by the will, he may charge the expense of such agent's salary to the estate; but in general he should not employ an agent in any transaction where he himself can act just as well. He will be allowed for all reasonable expenses and proper disbursements.

SECTION 30. Real Estate.—Unless real estate is devised to an executor in trust, the heir or devisee is the only person who has the right to its possession, except where it may be required to pay debts of the deceased, and the executor or administrator as such has no control over it; they receive their authority from the will or statute. Where a devise of real estate is made to an executor in trust to sell, etc., the title will vest in him, and he is accountable for the proceeds of such real estate upon such sale; but the executor should never think of selling any real estate without first consulting his counsel in relation thereto.

SECTION 31. Vouchers.—The executor or administrator should take vouchers for all payments made by him other than trivial expenses. His attention is directed to Section 12, under the head of "Trustees," and he should carefully read that section, as it applies to him in every particular. The following is a copy of Section 2734 of the Code of Civil Procedure, and is inserted here because of its importance:

"Section 2734. Upon an accounting by an executor or administrator, the accounting party must produce and file a voucher for every payment, except in one of the following cases:

"1. He may be allowed, without a voucher, any proper item of expenditure, not exceeding twenty dollars, if it is supported by his own uncontradicted oath, stating positively the fact of payment, and specifying when and to whom the payment was made; provided that all the items so allowed against an estate, upon all the accountings of all the executors or administrators, shall not exceed five hundred dollars.

"2. If he proves by his own oath or another's testimony, that he did not take a voucher when he made the payment; or that the voucher then taken by him has been lost or destroyed; he may be allowed any item, the payment of which he satisfactorily proves by the testimony of the person to whom he made it; or if that person is dead, or cannot after diligent search be found, by any competent evidence other than his own oath or that of his wife.

"But an allowance cannot be made, as specified in this section, unless the Surrogate is satisfied that the charge is correct and just."

Where an executor is also a trustee or guardian under the will, he should take a voucher in his capacity as executor, and another one as guardian or trustee on a payment to the ward or minor.

SECTION 32. Interest.—It is a general rule that legacies draw interest from the time that they are payable, and where no time is fixed by the will for the payment of a legacy it becomes due at the end of a year from the date of issuance of letters testamentary, and interest begins to run from that time. In some instances interest is to be computed from the date of the testator's death.

An executor or administrator will be charged with interest, which he must pay from his own private funds, when he mingles the funds of the estate with his own, retains them unnecessarily long, or in *any way* uses them for his own advantage. A reasonable time is allowed him in which to invest the funds; this time must vary according to the case. Generally six months from the date of the issuance of letters is considered sufficient, though a year is allowed where payments have to be made frequently; and interest will run against him generally after the lapse of eighteen months from the date of his letters.

SECTION 33. Sales.—Where the executor is given authority by the will to sell real estate, for any purpose, he may of course do so, either publicly or privately, and on such terms as the executor may deem for the best interest of the estate. He is of course accountable for the proceeds of the sale of real estate. Where real estate is devised to the widow until her death or remarriage, and then is directed to be sold, he has no authority in relation to such real estate until after her death or remarriage. Where real estate is directed to be sold for the payment of debts, that is the primary purpose to which its proceeds are to be applied, notwithstanding that the same property is devised to a devisee.

As to the personal property, the executor has general authority to sell it when necessary or advisable, and when directed by the will to sell it, for any purpose, he should sell it whenever he thinks he can obtain the highest price for it. He should always sell for cash only.

SECTION 34. Liability of one Executor or Administrator for the Acts of his Co-executor or Administrator.—The general rule that co-trustees are jointly and severally liable for each other's acts, does not apply to executors and administrators. Each executor is responsible only for the money and property he receives, and they each have equal right and authority to receive and pay out moneys individually, and without the knowledge or consent of the other; but this individual exemption does not always apply. For instance, one executor cannot wink at the fraud or improper acts of his co-executor. If he can be shown to have knowledge of, or in any way to have consented to, the wrongful acts of the other, he is responsible to the estate for any loss to it resulting from those improper acts. Where one executor or administrator knows that his co-executor or administrator is acting improperly with the estate, or any part of it, or refuses to do what he ought to do, in order to free himself from liability, he ought immediately request such wrong-doing executor to do his duty, whatever it may be, and if he does not comply with such request in a very short time, he should through his counsel apply to the Surrogate for an order in the premises. Each executor or administrator is bound to exert a watchful care over the estate, and prevent any loss to it by whatever means.

SECTION 35. Debts and Claims against the Estate.—An executor or administrator in many respects is a trustee for the creditors ; he should therefore pay only the funeral expenses attending the burial of the decedent, and should postpone the payment of all other debts until the expiration of the time limited in the notice to present claims against the estate. This applies to all cases where there is the slightest reason to suppose that the estate will prove insufficient to pay all the debts and claims against it in full, and if the executor or administrator pays claims in *full*, and subsequently and before the expiration of the time limited other claims are presented, such creditors may hold the executor or administrator personally liable for the amount of their claims or their proportional part of them. Where it appears that the estate cannot pay all the debts in full, they must be paid *pro rata*, and it therefore becomes necessary to know the amount of *all* the debts. To ascertain that, the statute authorizes the executor or administrator, after the expiration of at least six months since the granting of letters, to apply to the Surrogate for an order, authorizing him to insert a notice in a newspaper printed in the county and in such other newspapers as the Surrogate directs. The Surrogate ought to be informed by petition or otherwise where the creditors reside. This notice must be inserted once in each week for six months, "requiring all persons having claims against the deceased, to exhibit the same, with the vouchers thereof, to such executor or administrator, at the place of his residence or transaction of business, to be specified in such notice, at or before the day therein named, which shall be at least six months from the day of the first publication of such notice."

An excellent custom (among many others) now obtains in the office of the Surrogate of New York County, of sending notice to the executor or administrator after the lapse of six months, that he should advertise for claims. This notice when received should always be heeded, and whether received or not he should always apply through his counsel for an order to advertise immediately upon the expiration of the six months. The following are the prices charged at the present time for advertising this notice in the city of New York by the newspapers named : *The Daily Register*, office 303 Broadway, N. Y., the official law journal of the county, in which the notice is always advertised in proceedings in New York County, $20 ; *The Star*, $30 ; *The New York Evening Express*, $30 ; *The World*, $26 ; *The Commercial Advertiser*, $26 ; *The Daily News*, $20 ; *The Weekly Union*, of Morrisania, N. Y., $20 ; *The Hebrew Leader*, $20 ; *The Sunday Democrat*, $20. It is the almost invariable practice of the Surrogate to order the notice to be inserted in *two* newspapers. The clerk charges one dollar for notifying the executor or administrator of the time to advertise, entering the order, and supplying forms of the notice, which should be added to the charges of the two newspapers ordered, the *Daily Register* always being one. All these newspapers require payment in advance as a condition of their inserting the notice. After the expiration of the six months the executor should obtain and carefully preserve an "affidavit of publication" of the notice made by the publisher of the paper ; this will be needed on the accounting. The executor or administrator should always require claimants to produce the voucher, bill, or statement relating to their claims and verify or *swear* to it, but the claim need not be sworn to unless the executor demands it, and the executor or administrator has no right to *reject* or to refuse to receive and file any claim, statement, voucher (or scrap of paper which the creditor calls a claim or voucher), *because* it is not sworn to ; but he must receive and file it for what it is worth, having first requested the claimant to swear to it.

A claimant may file his claim after the expiration of the time limited in the notice to present, and in fact at any time up to the executor's or administrator's discharge after his last accounting ; but the claimant's right to have his claim *paid* upon its presentation after the expiration of the time named in the notice is another matter. Where there is no deficiency of assets, the claimant, if otherwise entitled thereto, is not debarred from having his claim paid, because presented after the time, and he may maintain an action against the executor to enforce payment. The object of the notice is to protect the executor and the estate, so that where a distribution takes place in full or *pro rata*, *after* the expiration of the time limited in the notice, all claims not presented by that time are not considered in the computation, and in case of a deficiency of assets claims not in the computation would not be paid.

If an executor owed the decedent a debt at the time of his death, or a liability accruing subsequently, that debt is not discharged because the executor was named as such in the will, the same as to an administrator ; but such a debt must be considered as a part of the estate the same as all others. If a debt is discharged by a will, such discharge does not hold good as against creditors, but is to be considered only as a specific legacy or bequest to the debtor. The executor or administrator can give no preference in any way to his own claim against the estate ; he must prove and verify his claim to the satisfaction of the Surrogate on the accounting, but he may and should prove it before the accounting. The Statute of Limitations may bar certain debts, including the executor's or administrator's own claim. A claim barred by the Statute of Limitations is not a "*just debt*" to an extent to authorize the executor to pay it without an order of the Surrogate. Section 2740 of the Code declares that from the death of the decedent until the first judicial settlement of an account of his executor or administrator, the running of the Statute of Limitations against a debt due from the decedent to the accounting party is suspended unless the accounting party was appointed upon the revocation of former letters issued to another person, and that after the first judicial settlement of the executor's or administrator's account the statute runs against his debt.

An executor or administrator has the statutory right to compromise or compound a debt due the estate, and he should do so when the interests of the estate require it. He should always obtain authority from the Surrogate to do it. But even in that event any party interested may show on the accounting that the debt was negligently or fraudulently compromised or compounded.

Where the personal property of an estate proves to be insufficient to pay all its debts, a creditor or the executor or administrator may apply to the Court for leave to sell real estate of the decedent for that purpose.

The first debts to be paid by an executor or administrator are the funeral expenses connected with the burial of the deceased.

These he can pay if reasonable in amount, without any order or authority, whether the estate is solvent or not, or he can pay them out of his own pocket and reimburse himself with the first funds he receives. The expenses of the deceased's last sickness, including the physician's bill, is generally paid among the first. If the estate can afford it, and creditors will not be injured, the erection of a tombstone over the decedent's grave is included as funeral expenses.

After the funeral expenses are paid, and a fund for the payment of the expenses of the administration is reserved, the debts *preferred by law* should be paid, in the following order of preference :

" 1. Debts entitled to a preference under the laws of the United States." (*All* debts due the United States are preferred, and the executor or administrator will be personally liable if the United States Government suffer any loss by a neglect to give such preference.)

" 2. Taxes assessed upon the estate of the deceased previous to death." (Such taxes only as were assessed upon the estate of the deceased at the *time of his death* are entitled to a preference ; assessments are not included in the term " taxes.")

" 3. Judgments docketed and decrees enrolled against the deceased, according to the priority thereof respectively." (Judgments are to be paid in point of time of their docketing ; judgments rendered in the courts of other States are not entitled to this preference ; the judgment must be against the *deceased*, and must have been entered before his death.)

" 4. All recognizances, bonds, sealed instruments, notes, bills, and unliquidated demands and accounts."

In certain cases the Surrogate may order the payment of rent, where it will benefit the estate, before debts of the fourth class. With this exception no preference can be given to any debt over others of the same class, except judgments in the third class, which are to be paid in the order of the time of their docketing. Debts due are not entitled to any preference over those not due ; such debts may be paid in their proper class, with a rebate of interest for the unexpired time. Judgments recovered *against the executor or administrator* are entitled to no preference over other debts of the same class.

Debts must always be paid before legacies ; they must be paid according to their legal priority from the proceeds of the sale of the personal estate, if there is insufficient collected from other sources. Property not specifically bequeathed should be sold first. The executor or administrator ought never to pay a debt in full, or a legacy, unless he is POSITIVE that the assets of the estate are abundantly sufficient to pay *all* the debts and legacies, or *all the debts* at least, *in full*, with a surplus for contingent expenses. Should there be insufficient assets to pay all in full, the unpaid creditors could compel the executor or administrator to pay their claim or the unpaid balance *from his own funds*. Where there is an insufficiency of assets to pay all debts, there must be a *pro rata* dividend paid in proportion to the amount of each debt, under the order of the Surrogate, upon all unpreferred and unsecured debts after deducting the amounts already paid on account, if any. After the expiration of six months after the granting of letters, any creditor of the estate may present a petition to the Surrogate for a citation to show cause, directed to the executor or administrator, why a decree should not be made for the payment of a debt or its just proportional part. It is in the discretion of the Surrogate to grant the application, and if there is reason to believe that the claim is not genuine it will be denied. The Surrogate cannot try the question of the validity or the proper amount of the claim.

Of course if the decree is granted the executor or administrator must obey it and pay the amount ordered therein.

A creditor acquires no lien against the estate because he has recovered judgment against the *executor or administrator*. The exact amount of the debt has simply been ascertained thereby. He cannot issue execution before the settlement of the executor's account without leave of the Surrogate.

If it appears that there are funds in the hands of the executor properly applicable to the payment of the judgment upon an accounting, the Surrogate will allow execution to be issued for the amount applicable.

If the claimant establishes his claim, and if an executor or administrator unreasonably refuses to pay a debt manifestly just and legal, and there is no deficiency of assets, he will be personally liable for the creditor's costs of proceedings to compel payment.

It is the duty of an executor or administrator to endeavor to collect debts owing to the estate by persons residing in other States and countries, if they are solvent; and he should procure himself or some other person to be appointed administrator in the State where the debt is to be collected. He is accountable for the amount of a debt which is lost by his neglect to collect it. If on the accounting it appears that there is a debt not due, and the creditor refuses to accept payment before due, with a rebate of interest, then there must be funds reserved to pay such claim.

The executor or administrator ought early to conclude whether to accept claims and pay them, or whether to reject any of them and refuse payment. He is personally liable for any invalid claim paid by him. He should never pay a claim barred by the Statute of Limitations without an order of the Surrogate (debts on simple contract are barred after six years from the time a right of action accrued on them).

Where a claim is disputed by the executor or administrator, he may agree in writing with the claimant to refer it to three disinterested persons, or to a disinterested person to be approved by the Surrogate; proceedings are had before the referee as on a trial, and a judgment may be entered and enforced thereon. An offer to refer a disputed claim must be made by the claimant. When a judgment for a sum of money only is rendered against an executor or administrator in an action brought against him in his representative capacity, where it appears: (1) that the plaintiff's demand was presented within the time limited by public notice; (2) and that payment was unreasonably resisted or neglected; or (3) that the defendant (the executor or administrator) refused to refer the claim; in either of these instances the Court may award costs against the executor or administrator, to be collected either out of his individual property, or out of the property of the decedent, as the Court directs, having reference to the facts which appeared on the trial. In all other cases and instances the executor or administrator is not personally liable for costs, unless the Court directs him to pay costs personally for mismanagement or bad faith in the prosecution or defence of the action. The executor should, in a case where he desires to do so. plainly inform the claimant that he refuses to refer his claim; but he is not deemed to have refused to refer until the claimant has offered to refer, and a refusal to refer will not be implied from a rejection of the claim. Where the executor disputes or rejects a claim exhibited to him after the commencement, and before the completion of the publication of the notice to present claims, unless the claim is referred, suit thereon must be commenced within six months after dispute or rejection, or within six months after a part of the debt becomes due. A failure to bring the action within the time named bars any recovery on the claim.

SECTION 36. Legacies.—Personal property is *bequeathed*, real estate is *devised*. Under a will, a *legatee* receives a *legacy* or *bequest* of *personal* property; a *devisee* receives a *devise* of *real* property or estate.

Legacies are of various kinds, as *general*, *specific*, or *demonstrative* as to subject matter; they are also either *vested* or *contingent*, *absolute* or *conditional*, as to the time and possibility of their enjoyment. A *general* legacy is one which does not relate to any particular thing or kind of property distinct from others of the same kind, and usually though not always refers to money. "To my cousin Rebecca Harris I give and bequeath the sum of ten thousand dollars," is a common instance of a general legacy. There is a general presumption of law that all legacies are general, and they are not to be considered as specific unless such clearly appears to be the testator's intention as expressed in his will. A *specific* legacy is one which distinctly names the object bequeathed, and separates it from the decedent's general property. For instance, to give "to my daughter Rachel, my gold watch, presented to me by the Spanish Government," is a specific legacy, and relates to that particular watch and no other; but if the testator had bequeathed to his daughter "a fine gold watch," he would then give a general legacy, and the executor would be authorized to purchase *any* "fine gold watch" and give it to the legatee. A *demonstrative* legacy partakes of the nature of both general and specific. A legacy is demonstrative when the particular fund, place, or property is designated from which it is to be paid or taken. For instance, "I give and bequeath to my son Abraham, the sum of twenty-five thousand dollars, to be paid to him from the proceeds of the sale of my New York

Elevated Railroad bonds, if they realize that amount," would be a demonstrative legacy.

The distinction between these different kinds of legacies is important to notice, for articles and property not specifically bequeathed are to be *first* sold for the payment of debts, should it become necessary to sell property for that purpose; and all the rest of the personal estate, including property bequeathed under a general legacy, must be so sold, and the proceeds applied before articles specifically bequeathed are to be taken. In case of a deficiency of assets after the debts are paid, legacies must be proportionately reduced—in other words, the legatee does not receive the whole of his legacy, but only a *pro rata* part of it. This reduction is called "abatement." In cases where it is necessary that there should be an abatement of legacies, the general legacies always abate, but specific legacies do not, because they cannot generally be the subject of decrease, but even *specific* legacies abate sometimes; but while specific legatees enjoy this exemption they are liable to be deprived of their legacy entirely, for if the legacy *fails* because the specific article bequeathed *does not exist* at the time of the testator's death, it is then said to have "*adeemed*," and the legatee loses the property bequeathed; as where the testator before his death sold or otherwise disposed of the property previously bequeathed; so also if by accident or otherwise the property bequeathed is not in existence; as if the testator were to bequeath "to my son David my ship 'Robinson Crusoe,' now on her way to New York from Halifax," and the ship should strike a rock and go down, the interest of the legatee would go down with her, and the executor would not be compelled to procure another ship for him. All legacies which are not specific or demonstrative are general. *Annuities* or bequests of money payable periodically are considered as general unless they are payable from the income of a certain specified fund, and then they become specific.

A legacy is "*vested*" where the right to its payment accrues immediately upon the death of the testator, and is "*contingent*" when the right of enjoyment rests upon the happening of some event. A legacy is "*absolute*" when it is bequeathed unqualifiedly, and is "*conditional*" when it depends upon the happening or not happening of some uncertain event by which it may accrue or be defeated. A "*residuary*" legacy is one to be paid after the payment and satisfaction of all debts and other legacies, and relates to any surplus there may remain undistributed by the will, including any property which was the subject of a "*lapsed*" legacy. A lapsed legacy is one where the legatee does not receive the property; in some cases, by reason of his death before the testator or otherwise; but the statute declares that a legacy to a *descendant* of a testator shall not lapse, but shall go to the legatee's children or other descendants.

Specific legacies should be paid or delivered before general legacies. Where the will contains no express declaration as to the priority of payment of legacies, any deficiency necessary to be supplied for the payment of debts and prior legacies is to be made up as follows: 1. From the residuary legacies. 2. From the general legacies. 3. From legacies given for a valuable consideration, as for the relinquishment of dower or any other right or interest. 4. From specific and demonstrative legacies.

Where the birth of a child is post-testamentary (or after the testator's death), the statute declares that such child is entitled to the same portion of his deceased parent's estate as would have descended, or have been distributed to him, if the parent had died intestate, and in such case *all* legatees, without exception, must contribute ratably to make up such child's share.

Where a legatee is also a subscribing witness to the will, and the will cannot be proved without his testimony, he is thereby disqualified from receiving his legacy; but if he would have been entitled to any share of the testator's estate in case the will was not established, he will be entitled to so much of the share that would have descended to him, as does not exceed the value of the devise or bequest made to him in the will, and he can recover the same of the devisees or legatees named in the will, in proportion to and out of the parts or portions devised and bequeathed to them.

Where a legatee is a minor (that is, under the age of twenty-one years), if the legacy is under fifty dollars in value it may be paid to his father, for the use of the infant legatee; but if it is of the value of fifty dollars or more, it can be paid under the direction of the Surrogate to a general guardian, only upon his giving security to the minor, to be approved by the Surrogate.

If there is no guardian the legacy is to be paid to the Surrogate to be invested by him for the minor's benefit.

The statute declares that no legacies shall be paid by any executor or administrator until after the expiration of *one year* from the time of granting letters testamentary or of administration, unless directed by the will to be sooner paid. As we have already stated, debts must always be paid before legacies, and one object of the statute requiring the elapse of one year before payment of legacies is that all debts and demands against the estate may be ascertained by advertisement, before the legacies are paid. The Surrogate may, in his discretion, make a decree directing an executor to pay a legacy or some part thereof, or an administrator to pay a distributive share or some part thereof, before the expiration of a year, upon the application of a person entitled to such legacy or share, where it is necessary for the support or education of the petitioner, and where it appears that the assets are sufficient to pay all debts, claims, legacies, etc., and one third over, upon the petitioner filing a bond approved by the Surrogate, conditioned that if any debts against the deceased shall duly appear, and which there shall be no other assets to pay, and there shall be no other assets to pay other legacies or shares, or not sufficient to pay all prior legacies and an equal share of those of the same class as the petitioner, that then the petitioner will refund to the executor or administrator the sum paid to him, or the proportional part thereof necessary for the payment of such debts, etc.

It is the frequent practice, and permissible under the statute, for the executor to pay to a legatee a part of his legacy, and an administrator to pay a part of a distributive share before the expiration of the year, but he always does so at his own personal risk. Where he does not require the legatee or distributee to apply to the Surrogate, and obtain an order directing the payment and the giving of the bond above mentioned (the bond may be required, although the will directs the payment before the year); but it is generally a matter resting entirely in the discretion of the executor or administrator; but he should never pay a legacy or debt, or even a *part* of it, until he is *positive* or reasonably certain that the estate will be sufficient to pay all prior debts and legacies, and legacies of the same class or a proportional part of them, as the one upon which the payment is asked to be made. If there is the slightest doubt about the ability of the estate to meet all claims and prior legacies, then the executor or administrator should compel the legatee or distributee to make application to the Surrogate.

Debts, legacies, or distributive shares, or any part of them, ought not to be paid by the executor or administrator until he has first consulted his counsel, as many questions arise which should be determined by the counsel and executor or administrator together, before any payments should be made.

After the expiration of one year from the date of granting of letters, where the estate is ample and after payments of all debts after due notice to present, the executor should deliver the specific legacies and pay the general legacies ; he may then be compelled by the Surrogate to do so, where there is no deficiency of assets, and an administrator may be compelled to pay a distributive share or a proportional part of it, after the lapse of the same period.

Any increase to a specific legacy goes with it. Dividends payable after the testator's death on stock bequeathed to the legatee go to the legatee.

Where a legatee or a person entitled to a distributive share of an estate owes the estate a debt, the executor or administrator may retain, offset, and deduct from such legacy or distributive share the amount of the debt due the estate ; if the amount of such debt is equal to the amount of the legacy or share, then the legatee or distributee receives nothing from the estate. Of course the executor's or administrator's acts in this respect must be finally confirmed by the Surrogate in the decree.

SECTION 37. Statute of Distribution.—An administrator must distribute the estate, after the payment of debts, according to the provisions of the statute relating to the distribution of intestates' estates.

The words " next of kin" denote those persons who under the statute become entitled, as relatives of the deceased, to share in his personal estate ; they do not generally include the widow or husband.

The Statute of Descent provides that " the real estate of every person who shall die without devising the same, shall descend in manner following: 1. To his lineal descendants; 2. To his father; 3. To his mother; and 4. To his collateral relatives;" subject in all cases to the rules and regulations thereinafter prescribed. We do not deem it necessary to here give the statute in detail, as we have heretofore stated that the administrator as such has no power over the *real* estate, which passes to the heir upon the death of the intestate, subject to his debts and other liens that may be on it.

In the Statute of Distributions of *personal* estate, the words "legal representatives" do not mean, as they usually do, the decedent's executors or administrators, but refer to children and grandchildren who take and stand in place of their deceased parent or grandparent. The portion of the estate which comes to a person under this statute is called "a distributive share."

If a child of the intestate should survive him, but should die before he receives his distributive share, his children or "next of kin" would not receive his share, but it would be payable to his executors or administrators; his right to the share having become vested upon the death of the intestate. The following is the statute:

"Where the deceased shall have died intestate, the surplus of his *personal* estate remaining after payment of debts, and where the deceased left a will, the surplus remaining after the payment of debts and legacies, if not bequeathed, shall be distributed to the widow, children, or next of kin of the deceased, in manner following:

"*Widow.*—1. One third part thereof to the widow, and all the residue by equal portions among the children, and such persons as legally represent such children, if any of them shall have died before the deceased.

"2. If there be no children nor any legal representatives of them, then one moiety (or half) of the whole surplus shall be allotted to the widow, and the other moiety shall be distributed to the next of kin of the deceased entitled under the provisions of this section.

"3. If the deceased leave a widow, and no descendant, parent, brother or sister, nephew or niece, the widow shall be entitled to the whole surplus; but if there be a brother or sister, nephew or niece, and no descendant or parent, the widow shall be entitled to a moiety of the surplus as above provided, and to the whole of the residue where it does not exceed two thousand dollars; if the residue exceed that sum, she shall receive, in addition to her moiety, two thousand dollars, and the remainder shall be distributed to the brothers and sisters and their representatives.

"4. *If there be no widow*, then the whole surplus shall be distributed equally to and among the children, and such as legally represent them.

"5. In case there be no widow, and no children, and no representatives of a child, then the whole surplus shall be distributed to the next of kin, in equal degree, to the deceased and their legal representatives.

"6. *If the deeeased shall leave no children*, and no representatives of them, and no father, and shall leave a widow and a mother, the moiety not distributed to the widow shall be distributed in equal shares to his mother and brothers and sisters, or the representatives of such brothers and sisters; and if there be no widow the whole surplus shall be distributed in like manner to the mother, and to the brothers and sisters, or the representatives of such brothers and sisters.

"7. If the deceased leave a father, and no child or descendant, the father shall take a moiety if there be a widow, and the whole if there be no widow.

"8. If the deceased leave a mother, and no child, descendant, father, brother, sister, or representative of a brother or sister, the mother, if there be a widow, shall take a moiety, and the whole if there be no widow; and if the deceased shall have been an illegitimate, and have left a mother, and no child or descendant or widow, such mother shall take the whole, and be entitled to letters of administration in exclusion of all other persons, in pursuance of the provisions of this chapter. And if the mother of such deceased shall be dead, the relatives of the deceased on the part of the mother shall take, in the same manner as if the deceased had been legitimate, and be entitled to letters of administration in same order.

"*Equal Degrees.*—9. Where the descendants or next of kin of the deceased entitled to share in his estate, shall be all in equal degree to the deceased, their shares shall be equal.

"*Unequal Degrees.*—10. When such descendants or next of kin shall be of unequal degrees of kindred, the surplus shall be apportioned among those entitled thereto according to their respective stocks, so that those who take in their own right shall receive equal shares, and those who take by representation shall receive the share to which the parent whom they represent, if living, would have been entitled.

"11. No representation shall be admitted among collaterals after brothers' and sisters' children.

"12. *Relatives of the half-blood* shall take equally with those of the whole blood in the same degree; and the representatives of such relatives shall take in the same manner as the representatives of the whole blood.

"*Born after.*—13. Descendants and next of kin of the deceased, begotten before his death, but born thereafter, shall take in the same manner as if they had been born in the life-time of the deceased, and had survived him."

Illegitimates.—By the Laws of 1855 illegitimates inherit real and personal property from their *mother*, as if legitimate.

Married women.—The Laws of 1867 declare that "the preceding provisions respecting the distribution of estates shall apply to the personal estates of married women dying, leaving descendants them surviving; and the husband of any such deceased married woman shall be entitled to the same distributive share in the personal estate of his wife to which a widow is entitled in the personal estate of her husband, by the provisions of this chapter, and no more."

Advancement.—Where the intestate in his lifetime pays any money to or makes any provision for any of his children, with the view of having such provision considered as a part of such child's ultimate share in his estate, such previous payment is called "advancement." The following is the law on the subject:

"If any child of such deceased person shall have been advanced by the deceased, by settlement or portion of real or personal estate, the value thereof shall be reckoned with that part of the surplus of the personal estate which shall remain to be distributed among the children; and if such advancement be equal or superior to the amount which, according to the preceding rules, would be distributed to such child as his share of such surplus and advancement, then such child and his descendants shall be excluded from any share in the distribution of such surplus.

"But if such advancement be not equal to such amount, such child, or his descendants, shall be entitled to receive so much only as shall be sufficient to make all the shares of all the children, in such surplus and advancement, to be equal as near as can be estimated.

"The maintaining or educating, or the giving of money to a child without a view to a portion or settlement in life, shall not be deemed an advancement within the meaning of the two last sections; nor shall those sections apply in any case where there shall be any real estate of the intestate to descend to his heirs."

SECTION 38. Account and Accounting.—There are accounts and accountings of various kinds in the Surrogate's Court; some are compulsory and others voluntary.

The account itself is merely a statement of the executor or administrator's receipts and payments, and all his proceedings and the disposition made by him of all property mentioned in the inventory, or which has come into his custody. To make that account effectual and binding as a statement of the representative's proceedings, there must be a judicial settlement of it by the Surrogate upon notice to all parties interested in the estate. Such an accounting is called a "final" accounting. It is called final not because it necessarily is the *last* one, but because the Surrogate adjudicates or judicially passes upon the account and the rights of all parties interested who have been notified that the accounting is to be a judicial settlement of the proceedings.

The accounting may relate only to the one or two parties who petition for it and the executor or administrator, in which case if the parties to whom it relates have been duly notified that it is to be judicially settled and passed upon by the Surrogate, it is as to them a "final accounting," and, as such, binding upon them as to all matters embraced in it; but a "final accounting" is most frequently had for the purpose of closing up the proceedings with a view to the executor or administrator being discharged from all liability, and the surplus being distributed among the parties entitled to it. Such an accounting must be upon notice to the widow or husband, legatees, next of kin, creditors, and *all* parties in interest, including a co-executor, or co-administrator, and they must be *duly* notified that a *judicial settlement* of the account is applied for, and that the accounting is to be a final accounting.

Under the new Code of Civil Procedure, an executor or administrator may at any time voluntarily file in the Surrogate's office an intermediate account, and the vouchers in support of the same.

The Surrogate may in his discretion make an order requiring an executor or administrator to render an intermediate account: Where a judgment creditor asks leave to issue an execution upon a judgment recovered against an executor or administrator, or upon a judgment recovered against the decedent in his life-time; or upon the return of a citation issued upon the petition of a creditor, legatee, or a person entitled to a distributive share in the decedent's estate, praying for a decree directing payment thereof; or where eighteen months have elapsed since letters were issued, and no special proceeding upon a petition for a judicial settlement of the executor's or administrator's account is pending.

The Surrogate may from time to time compel a judicial settlement of the account of an executor or administrator, upon the petition of a creditor, legatee, distributee, or any party in interest, in the following cases: 1. Where one year has elapsed since his letters were issued; but if the petition is presented in less than eighteen months from the date of letters, the order to account is not a matter of right, but is in the Surrogate's discretion. 2. Where his letters have been revoked or his powers have ceased. 3. Where he has disposed of real property under a decree authorizing him to do so. 4. Where he has sold any of the decedent's real property, or an interest therein, or has received any of the rents and profits of such real property. The executor must appear by counsel on the return of a citation issued on such a petition; and if no good reason exists why he should not then account, he should present his own petition (if one year has expired since his letters were issued), praying for a judicial settlement of his account, to the end that his administration may be closed and his proceedings wound up and himself discharged from all liability.

There may be several grounds of objection by the executor or administrator, showing why he should not account at that time; he may allege that the date has not expired after which he may be required to account, that the party petitioning for the accounting has no interest, that he has not collected all the assets, is about consummating the settlement of a large claim due the estate, that he has paid the applicant's claim, that an important suit in equity is pending, that the petitioner's claim is barred by the Statute of Limitations, etc.; but substantial reasons only will be regarded by the Surrogate.

At any time after the expiration of one year since letters were issued to an executor or administrator, he may present to the Surrogate's Court a written petition, duly verified, praying that his account may be judicially settled, and that *all* parties interested in the estate may be cited to attend the settlement. If one of two or more co-executors or co-administrators asks for a judicial settlement of his individual account he must pray that his co-executors or co-administrators be cited also. Upon the presentation of such a petition the Surrogate will issue a citation to all parties to attend the accounting, and upon the return of the citation he will take the account or refer it to a referee to take it, and hear the allegations and proofs of the parties respecting the same; any party may contest the account with respect to any matter affecting his interest.

Where an executor's or administrator's letters are for any cause revoked, he must always account. The Code of Civil Procedure declares that "To each account, filed with the Surrogate, as prescribed in this article, must be appended the affidavit of the accounting party, to the effect that the account contains, according to the best of his knowledge and belief, a full and true statement of all his receipts and disbursements on account of the estate of the decedent; and of all money and other property belonging to the estate, which have come to his hands, or which have been received by any other person, by his order or authority, for his use; and that he does not know of any error or omission in the account, to the prejudice of any creditor of, or person interested in, the estate of the decedent."

Upon the settlement of his account, an executor or administrator may prove any claim he may have against the deceased. The Statute of Limitations does not run against his claim during the period between the issuance of his letters and the first judicial settlement of his account.

Where there is a claim against the estate at the time of settlement which is unpaid, there must be a deposit of funds to meet it, if it is a valid claim.

Ancillary Administration.—This occurs where a foreign executor or administrator takes out letters within this county; his accounting here, as a rule, relates only to property which he holds to satisfy creditors' claims out of assets situated in this county. He accounts only for property which came into his possession here; the further administration of the estate is left to the court of principal administration, from which the executor was originally appointed.

SECTION 39. Commissions and Compensation.—The following is the statutory rate of commissions allowed to an executor or administrator: For receiving and paying out all sums of money, not exceeding $1000, at the rate of five per cent; exceeding $1000, and not amounting to $10,000, two and one half per cent; for all sums above $10,000, one per cent. Where the total account exceeds $5000, the rate is five per cent on the first $1000, two and one half on the next $9000, and one per cent on all above $10,000.

Although the statute declares that the commissions are to be allowed on all "*sums* of money" received and paid out, yet this has been held to include not only money, but also the amount and value of the property which passes through the executor's or administrator's hands, and that such value is the basis upon which the commissions are to be computed, so that where property is turned over to a party in interest, and accepted as a payment of money, the commissions are earned on the value of the property so transferred. In case of a mere transfer of the collected funds by one executor to another, the first executor is not entitled to commissions on the amount so transferred—the money must be received and paid out.

Commissions are not charged on each legacy paid. On the final accounting the commissions are to be computed on the total amount received and paid (or to be paid), after the commissions are deducted and the debts, and expenses of the accounting paid, the legatees or distributees are to receive the surplus.

Where moneys are reinvested, no commissions are allowed on such reinvestments ; if they were, the entire estate would be absorbed by commissions, and the law does not contemplate that.

Commissions are allowed only on the order of the Surrogate and upon a *settlement* of the account.

" Where the value of the personal estate of the decedent amounts to one hundred thousand dollars or more, over all his debts, each executor or administrator is entitled to the full compensation allowed by law to a sole executor or administrator, unless there are more than three, in which case the compensation to which three would be entitled must be divided equally among them." (Code, Section 2736.)

" But where the will provides a specific compensation to an executor or administrator, he is not entitled to any allowance for his services, unless by a written instrument filed with the Surrogate he renounces the specific compensation." (Code, Section 2737.)

" Where successive or different letters are issued to the same person, upon the estate of the same decedent, including a case where letters testamentary or letters of general administration are issued to a person who has been previously appointed a temporary administrator, he is entitled to compensation in one capacity only, at his election ; except that where he has received compensation in one capacity, he is entitled to the excess, if any, of the compensation prescribed by law in the other capacity, above the sum which he has already received." (Code, Section 2738.)

He cannot receive both the statutory allowance and the compensation given by the will, unless the will so declares ; if he desires he may renounce the compensation given by the will by a duly executed certificate filed with the Surrogate. In that case he would become entitled to the statutory allowance. If the testator should bequeath certain specific property to the executor in lieu of his commission, and that property should be lost or become valueless, the executor could not retain money of the estate as an equivalent. In the absence of fraud against creditors, the executor will receive both the statutory allowance and the specific compensation given by the will, if the will so declared.

Where the executor is also trustee under the will, he is not entitled to commission in both capacities, but he is entitled to commissions on all moneys *received* by him as executor, and on all his payments on final settlement of his account as executor of the fund, which he will thereafter hold as trustee.

Where there are several executors or administrators, commissions are to be computed not upon the amount received and paid out by each individually, but upon the total sum received or paid out by any or all of them.

Where the rate of compensation is increased by statute during the executor's administration, he is entitled to such increase upon an accounting had after the amendment was passed, although the services were rendered before the amendment.

An executor or administrator can receive no greater compensation or commission than the statute allows, no matter how much he may benefit and increase the value of the estate by his extra exertions.

The Surrogate may apportion the commission among the executors or administrators, according to the services rendered by them respectively.

ASSIGNEES FOR THE BENEFIT OF CREDITORS.

☞ *The attention of assignees is directed to all information and instructions under the head of " Trustees," as the matter there to be found is just as important to assignees as that contained under this title (which relates more exclusively to them) and is not repeated here simply to avoid repetition.*

SECTION 40. Taking Possession.—An assignee should, *immediately* after the assignment is recorded in the County Clerk's office, in the county in which the assignor resided or carried on business, proceed to take possession of the assigned estate; he should go in *person* to the assignor's place of business (and he should be lively about it, too; in a race between him and the sheriff he should always take " first money") and state to the person in charge that he is the assignee of the assignor for the benefit of creditors, and that the estate is now in his custody. He should leave one of his own clerks, or some person identified with himself, in charge of the assignor's place of business, if he cannot remain himself; and later he should remove the assignor's signboards, and should have his name " as assignee" printed on all letter-heads, etc.. It is a matter of great importance that this change of possession should be apparent, in order to aid in establishing the title of the assignee to the assigned property and estate, as against the sheriff acting under writs issued from the courts, at the suits of creditors and others. The assignee should take possession of all the assignor's property of any nature, real and personal, and in whatever form—that is, if the assignment conveys all the assignor's property; also all the assignor's books, papers, etc. The law requires an assignee of an assignor who assigns real estate situated in a county other than that in which the assignment was filed, to cause a certified copy of such assignment to be filed and recorded in the county in which such real estate is situated. This, of course, includes all other *States.* In some States, New Jersey for instance, the Recorder of Deeds will not accept for *record* a certified *copy* of the assignment ; in such cases the certified copy should be *filed* there, and the original assignment after it has been *recorded* correctly in the county where it was originally filed, should be taken from the file (this is allowed in New York County) and sent to the Recorder or Register of the county in the State where the real estate is situated, and there *recorded* or copied into his books of record, after which it should be returned to the file in its original county as a place of safety. In any county in the State of New York a certified copy will always be received by the Register or County Clerk for record. A certified copy of the assignment should always be recorded as a *deed* or *conveyance* in the office of the Register or County Clerk of the same county in which the assignment was originally filed, if the assignor has any real estate in that county. We recommend the assignee to have his counsel prepare deeds of any real estate belonging to the assignor, at the time of the assignment and executed at the same time as the assignment, or as soon thereafter as possible (as they can be prepared in a much shorter time than certified copies of the assignment can generally be obtained). These deeds should be sent to the office of the Recorder of the county where the property is situation, and there recorded. The fees for recording must be prepaid. The assignment itself or a certified copy may be sent afterward. Another advantage of sending the deeds is that the courts of another State *might* refuse to recognize the assignment under our laws, but they would regard the deed, if duly executed, as a valid transfer. Where property is situated in another State care should be taken to have the acknowledgment of the deeds conform to the laws of that State. They should be acknowledged before a commissioner for that State residing in this State, if possible. The assignment itself in such cases should be drawn, executed, and acknowledged in conformity with the laws of that State, as its sufficiency to transfer lands situated in another State is to be judged *solely* by the laws of the State where the real estate is situated. The assignee has no right to proceed to sell or dispose of the property until his bond is given. See Section 42, *post*.

SECTION 41. Schedules and Inventory. — If the schedules and inventory are filed by the assignor, they must be filed within twenty days after the *date* of the assignment (care should therefore be taken to always have the assignment dated the same day that it is *recorded*). If filed by the assignee they must be filed within thirty days from the date of the assignment. The assignee should always, whether the schedules are to be filed by the assignor or by himself, be sure to have the memorandum which is delivered to counsel, from which the schedules are to be prepared, contain : 1. The name, occupation, place of residence, and place of business of the assignor. 2. The name and place of residence of the assignee. 3. A full and true account of all the assignor's creditors, stating the last known address of each, giving the *street* and *street number* (this is necessary, as notices and citations have to be served in the course of the proceedings). If the creditor receive letters, etc., at his place of business, his business address should be given ; if he has no place of business, then the street and street number of his private residence should be stated. In the case of firms, their business address, *street and number*, is sufficient. These addresses *must* thus be given as to *each* creditor ; the memorandum should also state the exact sum of money owing to each creditor, with the true cause and consideration therefor, showing how the indebtedness was contracted, or what the debt is for, when (as near as possible) it was contracted, and a statement of any existing security held by the creditor for the payment of the same. 4. A full and true statement of all the assignor's property and estate at the date of the assignment, both real and personal, in law and in equity, with the mortgages or any other incumbrances existing thereon, and of all writings relating thereto. *Full details* and *particulars* must be given of the stock ; each lot must be described as to the number of pieces, yards, etc., or number of dozens, etc. ; and the nominal as well as actual value of such property, including the nominal and actual value of the outstanding debts according to the best knowledge of the assignor or assignee. These values *must* be stated, and the fact that it is sometimes difficult to arrive at them is never received as an excuse for not giving them. There should be two columns ; the nominal value should appear in one column, and the actual value in the next column on the same line. Properly these values should be given of each lot of goods or merchandise composing the stock, and of each outstanding debt due the assignor at the time of the assignment. The nominal value is considered to be the cost price of merchandise, and the face amount of the outstanding debt. The actual value is the amount which the lot of stock or outstanding debt is believed to be worth at the time of preparing the schedules. Of course no one can tell *positively* what the exact actual values are, but they must be estimated so as to come as near as possible, *however difficult* it may be ; care being taken, as before suggested, that the actual values are not *unnecessarily* and improperly high or above what they really ought to be, considering the manner in which the property is to be disposed of, and the assignee's conscientious duty toward the creditors.

The assignee should see that all discounts, and offsets, and deductions for goods returned, etc., are taken off in the schedule as to each lot or outstanding, as stated in the actual values.

The General Assignment Act of 1877, as amended in 1878, provides that any party in interest may apply for an assignee's removal, if he neglect, in case of a failure on the part of the assignor, to file an inventory and schedules within thirty days after the date of the assignment.

The rules of the Court of Common Pleas in regard to assignments require that each page of the schedules and inventory must be signed by the party filing (the assignor or assignee, as the case may be)—they should be signed at the bottom of the page ; and also that where the schedules are filed by the assignee there must be a full affidavit made by such assignee and some disinterested expert, showing the nature and value of the property assigned.

SECTION 42. Assignee's Bond.—The law declares that "The assignee named in any such assignment shall, within thirty days after the *date* thereof, *and before he shall have any power or authority to sell, dispose of, or convert to the purposes of the trust any of the assigned property*, enter into a bond to the people of the State of New York in an amount to be ordered and directed by the County Judge of the county where such assignment is recorded, with sufficient sureties to be approved of by such judge, and conditioned for the faithful discharge of the duties of such assignee, and for the due accounting for all moneys received by him, which bond shall be filed in the clerk's office of the county where such assignment is recorded (in the city of New York, in the office of the clerk of the Court of Common Pleas); but in case the debtor shall fail to present such inventory within the twenty days required, then the assignee, before the ten days thereafter shall have elapsed, may apply to said County Judge by verified petition for leave to file a provisional bond, until such time as he may be able to present the schedule or inventory as hereinbefore provided."

The rules before mentioned declare that the bond must be joint and several in form, and that at least one of the sureties must be a freeholder (that is, the owner of real estate within this State). Also that if the penalty of the bond be $20,000 or over, it may be executed by two sureties, justifying each in that sum, or by more than two sureties, the amount of whose justification united is double the penalty of the bond. (By justification is here meant the amount in value of a surety's property, either real or personal.)

Where the assignee is desirous of taking immediate possession of the estate, and disposing of the same, as where it is perishable, and he is unable to file his schedule, the Court will, upon the assignee's affidavit, in which must be fully set forth the property assigned, its nature, value, and extent, showing good reason, why the schedules cannot be filed, fix the amount of a temporary or provisional bond to be given by the assignee, and the amount of a final bond will be determined when the schedules are filed.

SECTION 43. Books of Account. — The rules read: "Every assignee shall keep full, exact, and regular books of account of all receipts, payments, and expenditures of money by him, which said books shall always during business hours be open to the inspection of any person interested in the trust estate." In his books he should also insert, at the time of filing, the names and addresses of claimants who file their claims with him, with the amount of the claim and the date of filing the same.

SECTION 44. Continuing Assignor's Business.—An assignee cannot lawfully continue the assignor's business; his only duty is to follow the directions given him in the assignment, *convert the assets into money, and make the payments directed.* In some *few* cases it may be shown that it will be of advantage to the estate generally to manufacture the stock on hand, but it is dangerous for him to do this; it may avoid the assignment, and he renders himself liable to be charged with wasting the assets. He had generally better sell the stock in its primary state as he finds it, without attempting to manufacture it, with other stock, into a completed state.

SECTION 45. Notice to Present Claims, etc.—The rules and practice of the Court of Common Pleas require that notice to creditors to present their claims against the assignor must be advertised and mailed in *all* cases, *whether a settlement or compromise has been effected by the assignor with his creditors or not*—that is, if the assignee desires to be discharged, and he should always desire that when his duties are ended.

The law declares that the judge may (and he always does in a proper case), upon the petition of the assignee, grant an order authorizing him to advertise a notice to creditors of the assignor to present to him their claims, with the vouchers therefor duly verified or sworn to, on or before a day to be specified in such advertisement, not less than thirty days from the last publication thereof, which advertisement or notice shall be published in two newspapers, to be designated by the judge in the order, as most likely to give notice to the person to be served, not less than once a week for six successive weeks (this is the usual time, and is sufficient); and if it appears by the assignor's books or otherwise (in which case it should be stated in the petition for the order to advertise) that any of the creditors reside out of the State of New York, then, in like manner, in the "State paper," which at present is *The Albany Morning Express*, office corner Green and Beaver Streets, Albany, N. Y. Its term as State paper expires March 8th, 1885. There is a regular form for this notice, which it is well to follow; it will be furnished by counsel. This notice, and all other notices in assignments in New York County, should always be advertised in *The Daily Register*, the official law journal of the county, office 303 Broadway, New York The other newspaper, two only being necessary where none of the creditors reside out of the State, is designated by the judge in the order, according to his preference, but *The Daily Register* is always named. The charge for inserting this notice in the usual form in the newspapers (payment in advance always being required) is as follows: *The Albany Morning Express*, $7.70; *The Daily Register*, $7 (if the assignee desires to be economical, a good trait in an assignee, this paper will print for him copies or "slips" of the notice at 50 cents per hundred); *The New York Evening Express*, $14.40; *The World*, about $12.60; *The Star*, about $14.40. These figures are liable to vary according to the size of the notice, a line or two making a difference of a dollar or two. The assignee should always send to the newspaper, when the advertisement is completed, for an affidavit of the publication of this or any other advertised notice. He should never forget to do this, as such affidavits are necessary on his accounting.

It is also required that a copy of this notice should be mailed to all creditors named on the assignor's books, at least thirty (30) days before the day mentioned in the notice for the presentation of claims. These and all other notices in assignment proceedings must be inclosed in a wrapper or envelope bearing a notice requesting the postmaster to return it to the sender, giving his name and address, within ten days unless called for. An affidavit of such mailing must be made and preserved and presented on the assignee's accounting, showing *by whom* the notices were mailed, *when*, and to all the creditors as required by the rule before mentioned; also showing the addresses to which they were sent. An affidavit must also be made showing what notices have been returned to the sender as undelivered.

SECTION 46. Payment of Claims.—An assignee should never pay a claim against the estate until it has been duly proven by the affidavit of the claimant duly sworn to before a notary public or other officer of like powers; but he has no right to refuse to receive and file a statement or memorandum purporting to be a proof of debt, because it is not sworn to. All claims before any payment is made thereon must be duly verified (*sworn* to), preferred and unpreferred. The attention of assignees is especially directed to this section, as the Court of Common Pleas, following a decision of the Court of Appeals, have recently decided that *only such claimants and creditors as duly prove their claims are entitled to share in the proceeds of the assigned estate.* The assignee should be careful not to pay *in full* any claim (except preferred claims), unless he has the funds on hand to pay all in full. Claims contracted by the assignor, however small, can have no preference unless preferred in the assignment.

The payment of all claims should be deferred until the assignee's accounting at the close of the proceedings, as the assignee for his own protection should have the Court (and referee on the accounting) pass on the validity and proper proof of claims. Where he pays a claim before the accounting, or any *part* of it, he does so at his own personal risk. In the great majority of cases, a *pro rata* payment only is all that the creditors receive. The amount of such payment cannot be determined until all the claims proven are considered, and all expenses are deducted.

A claimant may file his claim with the assignee after the expiration of the time limited in the notice to present, and in fact at any time up to the assignee's discharge after his last accounting ; but *after* the expiration of the time limited in the notice, if the assignee were to account immediately, and a computation made upon the amount of claims proven against the estate and allowed by the referee on the accounting, only those creditors whose claims were proven would be considered in the computation. In short, any claim filed at any time before the actual distribution of the assets by the assignee will be entitled to a dividend, if not objected to ; but where the claim is presented after the case leaves the referee on the accounting, the assignee should not pay dividend on it except by special order of the Court, as its validity must be passed upon.

SECTION 47. Payment of Preferred Claims.—He should be very careful in paying preferred claims to pay them in the *exact order* of preference set forth in the assignment, a failure to do this, with insufficient funds remaining to pay the injured creditors, would render the assignee personally liable to them. As this order of preference is sometimes a little difficult to determine where the preferences are in *classes*, the assignee should never pay a preferred claim until he has first consulted his counsel in regard thereto. He should obtain and always retain a certified copy of the assignment for his guidance. He should always remember the "reserve fund" mentioned in Section 19, under "Trustees," in paying preferred creditors.

The assignee should always compel a preferred creditor to swear to his claim, in the same manner as if he were unpreferred. This protects the assignment somewhat, the assignor in his oath to the schedule having sworn also that the claim was owing to the creditor.

In every assignment containing preferences the question arises, Can the assignee lawfully and safely pay the preferred claims immediately and before his accounting? The question is an important one. The circumstances attending each case are often so widely different that we are unwilling to consider that there is a fixed rule as to all cases, and we must therefore advise the assignee to consult his counsel. We will say, however, that the majority, if not all the decisions of the Court of Common Pleas, on the question are to the effect that the assignee *can* lawfully pay the preferred creditors before the accounting, if the assignment is unimpeached. Orders have been granted by that court upon the petition of a preferred creditor directing the assignee to pay the claim, because the assignment had not been attacked by a judgment creditor. The inquiries as to the good faith with which the assignment was executed, the genuineness of the preferred claim asked to be paid, and the probability or improbability of a successful suit by the judgment creditor to set aside the assignment, are all to be considered by the assignee before he pays a preferred claim. In most cases the assignees do pay preferred claims before the accounting.

SECTION 48. Selling the Assigned Property. — In making sales at auction (and that is the only way that an assignee should sell the property) the assignee must give at least ten days' notice of the time and place of the sale of personal property, and briefly describe the articles to be sold, being personal property, by advertisement in one or more newspapers (the ten days should be full and complete ; the last advertisement should be inserted before the tenth day prior to the sale); and he must give notice of the sale at auction of any real estate, at least twenty days before the day of such sale, the last advertisement being inserted more than twenty days prior to the day of the sale. Great care should be taken to observe all statutory requirements in the sale of real estate. The assignee must always sell by printed catalogues in parcels, and must file a copy of such catalogue, with the prices obtained for the goods sold marked thereon, with his final account.

He of course has a right to, and always should, obtain the services of an auctioneer. He can choose his own auctioneer. He should always advertise the sale of either real or personal property, wherever it may be situated, in the *Daily Register*, office 303 Broadway, New York City, the official law journal of the County of New York, and in such other newspapers as he may choose. It has been decided by one of the judges of the Court of Common Pleas in one case, that an advertisement inserted once in one newspaper is sufficient, but we recommend the assignee to advertise the sale of personal property once a week for at least two weeks, in at least two newspapers, and the sale of real estate twice a week for at least three weeks in at least two newspapers. Beside this advertisement he should always give notice by mail of any sale to all creditors, so that they may become purchasers if they desire.

If the property to be sold is situated in another county or State, he should advertise the sale in some newspaper published in that county or State. He should always make every effort to have the property realize as much as possible.

SECTION 49. Composition—Assignee's Accounting and Discharge.—An assignee who desires to have the assignment proceedings closed on *record*, and his bond cancelled, and his sureties relieved from liability, must account in *all cases, whether a compromise or settlement has been effected by the assignor with his creditors or not.* This is the rule and practice enforced by the Court of Common Pleas. And as he in some cases turns over the property in his hands to the assignor because of the composition or settlement, he should observe through his counsel that the composition papers are regular in form. At any rate, the

Court will not discharge him unless they are—that is, if he asks to be discharged, *because* the assignor has compromised with his creditors, and asks that the assignee deliver the property to him. The assignee should be particular, therefore, where a composition has been effected, to see that all the papers in the composition proceedings are carefully executed by the creditors themselves. A third party can execute them for a creditor only under peculiar circumstances, and the party signing should in such case show and swear to his authority; where a firm signs, the firm name should be signed by one of the firm, and under it the member who signed it should sign his own name, preceded by the word "by." All papers in composition proceedings should be under seal and duly *acknowledged* before and certified by a notary public or other officer of like powers, in proper form. It is better to have all the papers entitled in the assignment proceedings printed; of course these should be prepared in proper form by counsel. A voucher and release and consent to reconvey should be taken from each creditor.

It is a common practice, though it is actually unlawful and improper, in cases where the assignor has effected a composition or compromise with his creditors, for the assignee to advance him the money from the assigned estate wherewith to pay the composition payment—in other words, the assignor settles with his creditors upon the assumption that if they all sign the composition agreement, that he can immediately use the proceeds of the assigned estate to pay the amount in settlement. This he has no right to do until the Court grants an *order* directing the assignee to reconvey the assigned estate or its proceeds, and such order will not be made until the Court is satisfied that all the creditors have been paid or provided with the composition payment, and generally not until after the assignee's accounting. Where the assignee, before such an order is made, voluntarily delivers the assigned estate or its proceeds to the assignor, he does so at his own risk, for if the assignor under promise that he would pay his composition payment, should pocket the money, the assignee would be liable to the creditors for the value of the property so delivered. Therefore the assignee should be satisfied that the assignor will act honestly before delivering to him the property, and we recommend him to always pay the amount of the composition in such a case to the creditors himself. Of course the safer and better way is to proceed only on the order of the Court.

An assignee may petition the Court for leave to account at any time after the assignment is made. He may be *ordered* to account upon the petition of a creditor, the assignor, or the sureties on the assignee's bond, at any time after the lapse of one year from the date of the assignment, and he may be ordered to account when he is removed.

An assignee's account must be verified (sworn to). The affidavit is to the effect that the account, according to the best of the knowledge, information, and belief of the assignee, contains a full and true account of all his receipts and disbursements on account of the estate, and of all sums of money belonging to the estate which have come into his hands, or which have been received by any other person by his order or authority for his use, and that he does not know of any error or omission in the account to the prejudice of any of the parties interested in the estate.

Vouchers *must* be produced for all payments exceeding twenty dollars in amount, and we recommend him to take vouchers for smaller sums. Any item exceeding twenty dollars in amount for which no voucher is produced will be disallowed, in which case he must take the amount of it from his *own funds*. All items of disbursement under twenty dollars, for which he produces no voucher, will be allowed only when he swears *positively* (and not upon information and belief) that he paid them, to whom paid, when and for what purpose. The total amount of such items unsupported by vouchers must not exceed $500. See Section 12, *ante*.

SECTION 50. Assignee's Resignation or Removal.—An assignee may be removed on application of one or more creditors for misconduct or incompetency, and on his own petition showing sufficient reason therefor, upon five days' notice to the assignor, assignee's sureties, and to such other persons as the Court may direct. He must always account before he can be discharged, and then his bond will be cancelled.

SECTION 51. Assignee's Commission and Compensation.—The statute declares that "the assignee or assignees named in any assignment shall receive for his or their services a commission of five per cent on the whole sum which will have come into his or their hands."

Chief Justice Daly recently decided (*In re Hulbert*) that the five per cent above mentioned refers, as had been theretofore held, not only to money, but it also includes the amount and value of the property which passes through the assignee's hands, and that such value is the basis upon which an assignee's compensation is to be reckoned, and that in a case where the assignor has compromised with his creditors, and they agree that the assigned property may be returned to him, the total amount paid in composition or compromise, together with all expenses and payments by the assignee, is the proper value of the property assigned, upon which the assignee's commissions are to be computed. See Section 39 in regard to executor's commissions, which are governed to a certain extent, by the same practice as those of an assignee, but at a different *rate*.

RECEIVERS.

☞ *The attention of Receivers is directed to all information and instruction under the head of "Trustees," as the matter there to be found is just as important to receivers as that contained under this title (which relates more exclusively to them) and is not repeated here simply to avoid repetition.*

SECTION 52. Nature of the Office.—A receiver is an officer appointed by the Court, to take possession of, hold, control, and generally to dispose of certain property and its proceeds, under the order of the Court.

Probably the most common cases in which a receiver is appointed are where copartners are unable to agree, or where for any reason a dissolution is asked for. When a corporation becomes insolvent, a receiver is generally appointed upon the application of the attorney-general, and in any case where property the title to which is in dispute or the interest of parties entitled to it is undetermined and disputed, the Court, pending the question to be decided, usually appoints a receiver.

A receiver is also appointed where property of a judgment debtor is discovered upon his examination in supplementary proceedings.

A receiver is an officer of the Court appointing him, and he derives all his authority solely from the order appointing him and the practice of the Court as regulated by statutes, and acts entirely under the direction of the Court.

He represents *all* parties to the action or proceedings, and he should therefore be careful to always act impartially and without any favoritism to one party or the other.

He should never take any step in any matter of importance without first receiving the sanction of the Court by its order. He probably possesses less discretionary powers than any other trustee. His principal duty is, as his name implies, to *receive* money and property to be disposed of under the direction of the Court, though in some cases he is empowered to carry on the business of the parties who owned the trust property before his appointment.

Where a receiver is appointed in one action, he becomes thereby receiver of *all* the trust property, and represents not only the parties to the suit in which he was appointed, but also the parties to all subsequent suits relating to the same persons or property.

SECTION 53. Bond—Security.—A receiver must always give security, whether all the parties interested consent that he act without giving a bond or not.

The Code declares that "a receiver, appointed in an action or special proceeding, must, before entering upon his duties, execute and file with the proper clerk a bond to the people, with at least two sufficient sureties, in a penalty fixed by the Court, judge, or referee making the appointment, conditioned for the faithful discharge of his duties as receiver. And the Court, or when the order was made out of court, the judge making the order by or pursuant to which the receiver was appointed, or his successor in office, may at any time remove the receiver, or direct him to give a new bond, with new sureties, with the like condition."

Where the security given by the receiver become impaired by the insolvency of one of the sureties, or where additional property comes into his hands, he may, upon the application of a party in interest, be compelled to give additional security, in the shape of another bond with other or additional sureties.

The amount or penalty of the bond to be given by the receiver is fixed by the Court appointing him, when it has by affidavit or otherwise ascertained the value of the property as nearly as possible, that will come into the receiver's hands.

The bond must be executed by the receiver and two sureties, and is to the effect that the receiver will faithfully discharge the duties of his office, and promptly obey all the orders of the Court. Where the penalty of the bond is considerable, it may be executed by more than two sureties.

The receiver's appointment does not take effect until his bond has been duly approved and filed, and he cannot act until that is done.

The title to the trust property becomes vested in him immediately upon his giving the bond.

SECTION 54. Duties and Powers.—His first duty, after giving his bond, is to take possession of the trust property. This he may do without further order of the Court.

He may, where it is necessary, appoint a clerk or agent to assist him, but he should be careful not to make such an appointment if he can perform all the work himself; otherwise he may not be allowed for it upon his accounting, and then he would be obliged to lose the money paid to such agent or clerk. He should not pay any considerable sum without the order of the Court.

He must of course at all times protect the property and interests confided to his custody.

He becomes vested with the title to all personal property of the receivership immediately upon filing his bond, but he acquires title to real estate only by conveyance by direction of the Court. The party formerly in possession may be compelled to convey to him. The statute authorizes him to hold and dispose of real estate under the direction of the Court. All rights of action on contracts pass to the receiver, but claims for damages for personal torts, as for malicious prosecution, slander, libel, assault and battery, etc., do not, unless merged in judgment.

The following is a copy of Rule 78, one of the "General Rules of Practice" which have the same force as statutes: "Every receiver of the property and effects of the debtor shall, unless restricted by the special order of the Court, have general power and authority to sue for and collect all the debts, demands, and rents belonging to such debtor, and to compromise and settle such as are unsafe and of a doubtful character. He may also sue in the name of a debtor, where it is necessary or proper for him to do so; and he may apply for and obtain an order of course that the tenants of any real estate belonging to the debtor, or of which he is entitled to the rents and profits, attorn to such receiver, and pay their rents to him. He shall also be permitted to make leases, from time to time, as may be necessary, for terms not exceeding one year. And it shall be his duty, without any unreasonable delay, to convert all the personal estate and effects into money ; but he shall not sell any real estate of the debtor without the special order of the Court, until after judgment in the cause. He is not to be allowed for the costs of any suit brought by him against an insolvent, from whom he is unable to collect his costs, unless such suit is brought by order of the Court, or by the consent of all parties interested in the funds in his hands. But he may, by leave of the Court, sell such desperate debts, and all other doubtful claims to personal property, at public auction, giving at least ten days' public notice of the time and place of such sale."

The statute requires a judgment debtor to deliver to a receiver appointed in supplementary proceedings, any personal property which may be discovered belonging to such judgment debtor, and the receiver or any party in interest may apply for an order compelling such delivery, directed to the judgment debtor, if the property is in his possession, or to a third party who holds it. So also, the sheriff may be compelled to pay and deliver to such receiver all money and property in his hands belonging to the judgment debtor, after deducting his fees.

Where the proceedings in which the receiver was appointed are discontinued, or where the judgment has been satisfied, or where there is any surplus remaining in the receiver's hands after the satisfaction of the judgment, the receiver must, under the order of the Court *only*, pay and deliver to the judgment debtor or other person entitled to it, such property or surplus, upon the payment of his fees, and all other sums legally chargeable against the same.

A receiver appointed upon the death of a sole surviving executor has the same powers as the deceased executor. A receiver of a creditor of an insolvent's estate may consent to the insolvent's discharge, when *ordered* to so consent by the Court.

The new Code declares : That an order appointing a receiver of the property of a judgment debtor in supplementary proceedings, or extending the receivership (as where a judgment creditor in a second suit asks for the appointment of a receiver ; in such case the powers of the receiver originally appointed are extended to the parties and property in or relating to such second or subsequent suit) must be filed in the office of the clerk of the county wherein the judgment roll in the action is filed; or if his appointment is based upon an execution issued out of a court other than that in which the judgment is rendered, in the office of the clerk of the county wherein the transcript of the judgment is filed.

The property of the judgment debtor is vested in the receiver, who has qualified (or given his bond) from the time of filing the order appointing him or extending the receivership, except that real estate is vested in him only from the time when the order, or a certified copy thereof, as the case may be, is filed with the clerk of the county where it is situated. Where the judgment debtor resides in another county of the State, a certified copy of the order appointing the receiver must be filed in the county where the judgment debtor resides.

It is a general rule that the receiver's title relates back to the date of serving an order or warrant upon any party in relation to any of the property of the judgment debtor.

The receiver is responsible for any loss that may result from his neglect in the care and management of the estate.

He may apply to the Court for instruction in regard to the care and management of the estate, and, as we have before stated, he always should do so when any question of importance arises.

SECTION 55. Suing and Being Sued.—"Whenever a receiver, appointed under proceedings supplementary to execution, shall apply for leave to bring an action, he shall present and file with his application the written request of the creditor in whose behalf he was appointed, that such action be brought; or else he shall give a bond with sufficient security and properly acknowledged and approved by the Court, to the person against whom the action is to be brought, conditioned for the payment of any costs which may be recovered against such receiver And leave to bring action shall not be granted except on such written request, or on the giving of such security.

"In all other cases where a receiver applies to the Court for leave to bring an action, he shall show in such application that he has sufficient property in his actual possession to secure the person against whom the action is to be brought for any costs which he may recover against such receiver ; otherwise the Court may require the receiver to give such bond conditioned for the payment of costs, and with such security as is above mentioned."

"No receiver shall have power to employ more than one counsel, except under special circumstances and in particular cases requiring the employment of additional counsel, and in such cases only upon special application to the Court, showing such circumstances by his petition or affidavit, and on notice to the party or person on whose behalf or application he was appointed. This rule shall apply to all receivers, present and future ; and no allowance shall be made to any receiver for expenses paid, or made, or incurred in violation of this rule."

The two foregoing rules of the courts shall always be carefully heeded by the receiver.

He should never bring proceedings of a criminal nature, as where he applies to have the defendant in an action brought by him, arrested, unless he not only receives the written request of the creditor for whom he is acting, but a very substantial bond with good sureties from such creditor, to the effect that he will indemnify the receiver for any loss or damage he may sustain ; for if the receiver should be unsuccessful the injured defendant could bring an action against the receiver personally, and charge him personally, not only for the costs, but also for *damages*, for false imprisonment, etc. He should never in any event bring such an action except upon the recommendation of competent counsel, and unless he is well protected by a bond and the order of the Court.

Being an officer of the Court it is contempt of Court to sue a receiver without permission of the Court appointing him, and, on the other hand, he must obtain the leave of the Court to bring an action against some one else ; if he does not do so he will be personally liable for costs.

In an action brought by a receiver, the Court may, in its discretion, require him to give security for costs.

See Rule 78, quoted near the beginning of the previous Section 54, *ante*.

He should generally obtain leave to defend an action brought against him as receiver.

SECTION 56. Continuing Business, etc.— He should proceed to collect the outstanding debts due the estate, and sell the property without delay. He may in some cases be justified in carrying on the business for a brief period in order to sell the property at a better price ; but he should be careful not to continue it too long, as the Court will not continue the business longer than is necessary to prevent a sacrifice of the property.

SECTION 57. Sales.—He should convert the personal estate into money. He may obtain an order authorizing him to sell doubtful claims. He should always sell the property by auction, giving at *least* ten days' notice of the sale of personal property, the notice should be advertised once a week for three weeks in two newspapers, generally designated by the Court in the order, *The Daily Register*, official law journal of New York County, always being one in sales in this county.

SECTION 58. Inventory.—He should always make and file an inventory of all the property which comes into his hands, with its appraised value. He should file one at the commencement of the proceedings, and at any time after when property comes into his hands. This he should do not only for his protection, but also for his convenience on his accounting.

SECTION 59. Accounting.—The rules formerly required him to make and file an annual account or report, and it is an advantage for him to do so, where the estate is large and his administration continues for several years.

Of course when his administration is closed, and the proceedings are ended, he must always account to the Court before he can be discharged. He first has his account showing all his receipts and expenses prepared and filed, and he then petitions the Court for an accounting upon notice to all parties interested. The accounting is then referred to a referee, who examines the account and the receiver, and takes testimony and reports to the Court, upon which a decree is entered discharging the receiver and his sureties if everything is satisfactory.

He should always give notice of his appointment by mail and advertisement, and require claimants to verify their claims within a fixed day, or be barred from sharing in a dividend to be paid at that time, if any. He should always give three weeks' notice of the payment of a dividend.

SECTION 60. Compensation—Commissions.—Section 3320 of the Code of Civil Procedure reads: "A receiver, except as otherwise specially prescribed by statute, is entitled, in addition to his lawful expenses, to such a commission, not exceeding five per centum upon the sums received and disbursed by him, as the Court by which, or the judge by whom, he is appointed allows."

The commissions are computed not only upon money, but on the value of the property which passes through the *receiver's* hands in place of money.

One of the exceptions provided for in the above section is that of a receiver of a *moneyed corporation*, who, by the Laws of 1842, is allowed the same commissions as are allowed by law to an executor or administrator—viz. : For receiving and paying out all sums of money, not exceeding $1000, at the rate of five per cent; for receiving and paying out any sums exceeding $1000, and not amounting to $10,000, at the rate of two and one half per cent; for all sums above $10,000, at the rate of one per cent.

SECTION 61. Receivers of Corporations.—A receiver of a corporation becomes vested with all the estate, real and personal, of the corporation from the time of filing the required security.

He must immediately give notice of his appointment by advertising—"once a week for three weeks," the statute says; but he should always continue it for six weeks so as to give ample notice. The notice should be published in the State paper, now *The Albany Morning Express*, published at Albany, and in at least two newspapers published in the county in which the principal place of business of the corporation is situated, and also by mail to *all* parties interested. The notice should be to the effect that the receiver was duly appointed by the Supreme Court, and that pursuant to an order of the Court, notice is given to all persons having claims against the corporation to present them within a time in the notice, which should be at least two months from the date of the last publication of the notice. The notice should also require any debtor to the corporation to pay to him any debts or claims owing to it and deliver to him any property belonging to the corporation.

He should also always give full and lengthy notice of the payment of any dividend to all stockholders, creditors, claimants, etc.

He should compel any subscribers to the capital stock of the corporation who have not paid for their shares, to do so, and for that he may, if necessary, and by leave of the Court, bring an action against them.

He must call a meeting of all creditors of the corporation within four months after his appointment, and make to them at such meeting a statement of all his receipts and disbursements, and his balance on hand, and of all open and subsisting contracts with the corporation, and in certain cases he is authorized to cancel such contracts.

He must pay all claims and demands against the corporation according to the order of preference given by the statute, which we do not give here for the reason that it is presumed that the receiver of a corporation will *constantly* consult his counsel, as the interests involved in such cases are of such magnitude that the right to pay each particular claim or class of claims, and to do any act generally, is to be carefully considered by his counsel.

Generally, two dividends are to be paid, of both of which full notice should be given by advertisement and by mail to all parties in interest.

Within three months after the payment of the final dividend, the receiver must account. Notice should be given by publication of the time and place of accounting.

GUARDIANS.

☞ *The attention of Guardians is directed to all information and instruction under the head of "Trustees," as the matter there to be found is just as important to guardians as that contained under this title (which relates more exclusively to them), and is not repeated here simply to avoid repetition.*

SECTION 62. Nature of the Office.—A guardian is a person who by law has the custody of the person and estate of an infant (and an infant, as we have previously stated, is, in this State, any person, male or female, under the age of twenty-one years ; in the Surrogate's Court an infant is generally called a minor, after the Civil law ; various rights accrue to the infant upon his attaining the age of fourteen years, the principal of which is that he is then allowed to nominate his own guardian). A person who is under the care of a guardian is called a ward.

A guardian, unless he sooner resigns or is removed, continues his protective care of his ward until the ward arrives at majority (twenty-one years of age). The relation of guardian and ward during this period closely resembles that of parent and child, though the guardian's duties are not exactly similar to a parent's. The guardian is not compelled to support the infant, except from the child's own estate, and he has no right to the ward's services. An infant's parents are his guardians by nature.

In this State, where an infant acquires real estate, the guardianship belongs, *first*, to the father ; *second*, to the mother ; and *third*, to the nearest and eldest relative of full age, males being preferred to females.

But the appointment of a *testamentary* guardian appointed by the Court, supersedes the guardians just mentioned.

The Supreme Court has the inherent power to appoint a general guardian, and it acts as guardian of all infants (the ward is allowed his choice if over fourteen) ; and that Court may require the guardian to account at any time for all money and property belonging to the ward.

A testamentary guardian is appointed by a father's will (a guardian may also be appointed by deed), but the written consent of the mother is necessary to such appointment, although there is a decision to the effect that such consent is not necessary since the Law of 1871. In case of the omission of the father to make such disposition of the child, its mother may do so in like manner.

The same person is usually appointed guardian of both the person and estate of the ward.

The Surrogate may also appoint a general guardian, upon the application of any person in the infant's behalf, if under fourteen, and upon the petition of the infant himself if over fourteen, who at that age has the right to nominate his own guardian, to be appointed by the Surrogate ; and upon the application for probate of a will, as to which infants are interested parties, and also upon the accounting of an executor or administrator, the Surrogate appoints a *special* guardian to look after the interests of infants in the proceedings.

And when an action is about to be brought by or against an infant, the Court (or a *judge* under the new Code, except in a partition suit, when the appointment must be made by the *Court*) appoints a person to prosecute or defend the action for the infant ; such a person so appointed is called a "guardian *ad litem*" (that is, for the suit).

SECTION 63. Powers and Duties.—A general guardian, unless he sooner resign or is removed, continues his duties and protective care and custody of his ward until the latter reach his majority (that is, the age of twenty-one years).

The guardian has almost the same power and authority over his ward that the father has. He has the care and custody of the ward's person and property (if appointed guardian of both his person and estate, which is usually the case, though there may be a separate guardian for each). He may direct his education, and change his place of residence, and supervise his religious and moral instruction. The guardian is not entitled to the ward's earnings for his services; and on the other hand he is not responsible for the ward's debts for necessaries beyond the value of the ward's estate in his hands.

Guardianship of the person of a female generally ends when the ward marries, and in case of females guardianship of the property also, though if the deed or will of the parent should provide for such marriage before majority, and declare that notwithstanding the guardianship should continue during infancy, it is probable that marriage during minority would *not* end the guardianship.

Decisions in this State are to the effect that the marriage of a male infant does not end the guardianship.

The guardian appointed by order of the Court cannot consider himself released except by order of the Court.

A person appointed guardian of the person and property of an infant, by an infant's parents, in a last will and testament or a deed executed by such parents, and where such parent shall have died after September 1st, 1880, cannot exercise within this State any of the powers or duties of such guardian, "unless the will have been duly admitted to probate, and recorded in the proper Surrogate's Court, and letters of guardianship have been issued to him thereupon; or by virtue of an appointment contained in a deed of the infant's father or mother, being a resident of the State, unless the deed has been acknowledged or proved, and certified so as to entitle it to be recorded, and has been recorded in the office for recording deeds in the county in which the person making the appointment resided at the time of the execution thereof. Where a deed containing such an appointment is not recorded within three months after the death of the grantor, the person appointed is presumed to have renounced the appointment; and if a guardian is afterward duly appointed by a Surrogate's Court, the presumption is conclusive." (Code, Section 2851.)

Where a will was admitted to probate after September 1st, 1880, before letters are issued to the guardian, before he can enter upon the discharge of his duties, he must within thirty days thereafter (after the probate of the will), or within such further time as the Surrogate may allow, not exceeding three months, take an official oath before the Surrogate, a notary public, or officer having power to administer oaths to be used in the Supreme Court, to the effect that he will well, faithfully, and honestly discharge the duties of his office as such guardian, and the same must be filed with the Surrogate appointing him.

A person appointed guardian by will may, at any time before he qualifies, renounce the appointment by a written instrument under his hand, filed in the Surrogate's office.

The Surrogate's Court has jurisdiction "to appoint and remove guardians for infants; to compel the payment and delivery by them of money or other property belonging to their wards, and in the cases specially prescribed by law, to direct and control their conduct, and settle their accounts."

The guardian must carefully preserve and keep in good condition all the ward's property, real and personal, and if necessary, he may expend from the income of the estate funds for that purpose, and must deliver the property, and all its unexpended income and increase, to the ward when he comes of age, at which time he must also account to him for all the property and estate which has come into his hands as such guardian. If he makes or suffers any waste, sale, or destruction of the inherited real estate, he will lose the custody of the same and of the ward, and shall forfeit to the ward twice the sum at which the damages shall be taxed by the jury.

Section 2846 of the Code is as follows: "Upon the petition of the general guardian of an infant's person or property, or of the infant, or of any relative or other person in his behalf, the Surrogate, upon notice to such persons, if any, as he thinks proper to notify, may make an order directing the application by the guardian of the infant's property, to the support and education of the infant, of such a sum as to the Surrogate seems proper, out of the income of the infant's property, or, where the income is inadequate for that purpose, out of the principal."

As a matter of precaution, the guardian should always obtain the sanction of the Court by its order, of the amount of the income or principal which he shall expend in the education and support of the ward, and this too even where the instrument by which he was appointed fixes the amount.

He should *never* use the principal or sell the infant's real estate without an order of the Court authorizing him to do so.

All courts maintain a jealous watchfulness over the rights of infants, who are presumed to be ignorant of business affairs and generally helpless ; consequently a guardian should always act with great prudence, and after mature deliberation as to the best course to pursue for the infant's welfare.

SECTION 64. Bond and Security.—A general guardian of an infant's property, before he receives his letters, and before he may lawfully do any act in his official capacity, must execute a bond, besides taking his official oath, to the infant, with at least two sureties, in a penalty to be fixed by the Court, not less than twice the value of the personal estate of the ward and of the rents and profits of the real property. Each of the sureties must be worth the amount of the penalty of the bond over and above all his debts.

By the Laws of 1881 the Surrogate is empowered to take a bond of a guardian for double the amount of three years' income from real property to which an infant may be entitled, in his discretion.

Where the guardian is appointed by the Supreme Court, the Court may in its discretion vary the security, where from special circumstances it may be found for the interest of the infant ; and may direct the principal of the estate, or any part thereof, to be invested in the stocks of the State of New York, or of the United States, or with the New York Life Insurance and Trust Company, the United States Trust Company, the Union Trust Company, the Brooklyn Trust Company, or the Farmers' Loan and Trust Company, and by rule adopted, July 25, 1881, in the Central Trust Company, which is now made a regular court depositary to the extent of the above-named companies ; or on bond and mortgage upon unincumbered improved property of at least double the value of the amount invested, to be shown to the satisfaction of the Court, for the benefit of the infant, and that the interest or income thereof only be received by the guardian.

The condition of the bond is, that the guardian will, in all things, faithfully discharge the trust reposed in him, and obey all lawful direction of the Court touching the trust; and that he will in all respects render a just and true account of all money and other property received by him, and of the application thereof, and of his guardianship, whenever he is required so to do, by a court of competent jurisdiction.

The Surrogate may also require a guardian of an infant's person to execute a bond to the infant in a penalty to be fixed by the Surrogate, with or without sureties, conditioned that the guardian will faithfully perform all his duties, and account for all moneys which may come into his hands.

SECTION 65. Account and Accounting.—As we have before stated, the Supreme Court has jurisdiction over all guardians, and it may require them to account at any time.

The Surrogate may compel a guardian appointed by him to account in the following cases only:

"1. By the ward, after he has attained his majority.

"2. By the executor or administrator of a ward who has died.

"3. By the guardian's successor, including a guardian appointed after the reversal of a decree, appointing the persons so require to account." (Code, Section 2847.)

This refers to a "judicial settlement" of the account, and is distinct from the annual account required to be filed by the guardian, which we shall presently refer to.

The Surrogate may also, where the guardian was appointed by the Supreme Court, require him in like cases to account.

The following is a copy of Section 2842 of the Code of Civil Procedure: "A general guardian of an infant's property, appointed by a Surrogate's Court, must, in the month of January of each year, as long as any of the infant's property, or of the proceeds thereof, remain under his control, file in the Surrogate's court the following papers:

"1. An inventory, containing a full and true statement and description of each article or item of personal property of his ward, received by him since his appointment, or since the filing of the last annual inventory, as the case requires; the value of each article or item so received; a list of the articles or items remaining in his hands; a statement of the manner in which he has disposed of each article or item not remaining in his hands;

and a full description of the amount and nature of each investment of money made by him.

"2. A full and true account in form of debtor and creditor, of all his receipts and disbursements of money, during the preceding year; in which he must charge himself with any balance remaining in his hands, when the last account was rendered, and must distinctly state the amount of the balance remaining in his hands, at the conclusion of the year, to be charged to him in the next year's account."

A guardian appointed by will or by deed may also be *required* to file such account upon the application of any party in interest, by the Surrogate's order.

This annual account is carefully examined by the Surrogate, and is required so that he and the ward may know the condition of the estate.

An affidavit must be annexed to such account, which must state in substance "that the inventory and account contain, to the best of the affiant's knowledge and belief, a full and true statement of all the guardian's receipts and disbursements, on account of the ward; and of all money and other personal property of the ward, which have come to the hands of the guardian, or have been received by any other person by his order or authority, or for his use, since his appointment, or since the filing of the last annual inventory and account, as the case requires; and of the value of all such property; together with a full and true statement and account of the manner in which he has disposed of the same, and of all the property remaining in his hands at the time of filing the inventory and account; and a full and true description of the amount and nature of each investment made by him since his appointment, or since the filing of the last annual inventory and account, as the case requires; and that he does not know of any error or omission in the inventory or account to the prejudice of the ward."

It will thus be seen that guardians are held to a strict account, but if they regulate their acts by the requirements of the foregoing oath, they will comply with the statute, and do all that can be required of them.

A failure to file such annual account will subject the guardian to removal from office, and where the account filed by him is not full and complete, or is erroneous, he may be compelled to amend it, and file an additional and further account, he must file such account where he has not filed it, or he must file a more detailed account when required, within three months after the service upon him of the order of the Surrogate requiring him to file such account.

The guardian of an infant's *person* may also be required to account when he is shown to have received money or property of the ward for which he has not accounted.

The guardian himself (of either the infant's person or property) may present to the Surrogate's Court a written petition duly verified, praying for a judicial settlement of his account in the three cases before mentioned where he may be *required* to account, and he may at the same time ask for a discharge from his duties and liabilities.

The requirements in regard to vouchers, and the proceedings generally on the accounting, are the same as those relating to an executor or administrator.

SECTION 66. Commission and Compensation.—A guardian is entitled to the same compensation as is allowed by law to executors and administrators. See Section 39, under the head of "Executors and Administrators." A guardian is allowed commission on all receipts and payments of money by him during the year, where he renders an annual account, as he is now compelled to do by statute.

Upon filing his first annual statement or account, he is allowed one half of the commissions stated in Section 39 above mentioned, upon all moneys received by him, and half commissions on all moneys paid out by him (other than moneys invested or reinvested by him in securities, leaving the balance of his half commission to be computed upon the fund which has come into his hands, and which remains invested or unexpended at the time of the accounting, for future adjustment when expended, or when finally accounted for; and upon subsequently filing his annual account, half commissions are to be computed in the same manner upon all sums received as interest or income, or as additions to the capital of the estate, since the last account was filed, and half commissions upon all sums expended, except as investments.

SECTION 67. Removal from Office.—The Surrogate is empowered, by Section 2832 of the Code, upon the application of a party in interest, the ward or any one in his behalf, or the guardian's surety, to remove the guardian from office, for the following causes :

"1. Where the guardian is disqualified by law, or is, for any reason, incompetent to fulfil his trust.

"2. Where, by reason of his having wasted or improperly applied the money or other property in his charge, or invested money in securities unauthorized by law, or otherwise improvidently managed or injured the real or personal property of the ward, or by reason of other misconduct in the execution of his office, or his dishonesty, drunkenness, improvidence, or want of understanding, he is unfit for the due execution of his office.

"3. Where he has wilfully refused, or without good cause neglected to obey any lawful direction of the Surrogate contained in a decree or an order ; or any provision of law relating to the discharge of his duty.

"4. Where the grant of letters to him was obtained by a false suggestion of a material fact.

"5. Where he has removed, or is about to remove, from the State.

"6. In the case of the guardian of the person, where the infant's welfare will be promoted by the appointment of another guardian."

So the *guardian* may petition to have his letters revoked, his account settled, and himself discharged ; but the Surrogate may in his discretion entertain or decline to entertain the application.

SECTION 68. Guardian ad litem.—The Code declares that where an infant has a right of action he is entitled to maintain it, and being too young, presumably, to properly look after his own interests in the course of the litigation, the Court appoints a guardian *ad litem*, for him for that purpose.

SECTION 69. Bond and Security of Guardian ad litem.—A guardian *ad litem* appointed for an infant is not permitted to receive money or property of the infant other than costs or expenses allowed to the guardian by the Court, until he has given sufficient security approved by a judge of the court or a county judge, to account for and apply the same under direction of the judge. The security must be a bond to the infant in such penalty as the judge directs, not less than twice the sum or value of the property to be received, executed by the guardian and two sureties, approved and filed with the clerk of the court.

This does not apply to the general guardian of an infant who has been appointed guardian *ad litem* (a guardian *ad litem* is always appointed in an action by or against an infant, whether there is a general guardian or not); but the Court *may* require the general guardian to give additional security; but in an action for partition of an infant's real property, even a general guardian must *always* give a bond.

SECTION 70. Miscellaneous Duties and Liabilities.—A guardian *ad litem* should mark on the front of all legal papers served upon him the exact date when they were served, and he should then immediately send or take them to his counsel. Delay may be injurious alike to the guardian and the infant.

A guardian *ad litem* for an infant *plaintiff* is by statute made responsible for the costs of the action; such costs range in amount from $100 to $500, according to the amount in dispute and the intricacy of the question involved; a guardian for an infant defendant is not liable for costs unless specially charged therewith by the order of the Court for personal misconduct.

The written consent accepting the appointment of a guardian *ad litem*, except the clerk of the court, must always be produced to the Court or judge making the appointment.

COMMITTEES OF LUNATICS, IDIOTS, AND HABITUAL DRUNKARDS.

☞ *The attention of Committees is directed to all information and instruction under the head of "Trustees," as the matter there to be found in just as important to committees as that contained under this title (which relates more exclusively to them), and is not repeated here simply to avoid repetition.*

SECTION 71. Nature of the Office.—Formerly the care and custody of the persons and the property, both real and personal, of lunatics, idiots, persons of unsound mind, and persons who are incapable of conducting their own affairs in consequence of habitual drunkenness, was vested in the Chancellor of the State.

But since the office of Chancellor was abolished, the same powers which he possessed are now vested in the Supreme Court and in the various County courts of the State, including the Court of Common Pleas for the City and County of New York, where the lunatic resides in that county, and each of these courts now has the power to appoint a committee of the person and estate of a lunatic or similarly incapable person.

A committee (this word, although a collective noun, and generally denoting more than one person, is in this connection usually employed to designate but a single individual) of course must himself or herself (a female, married or unmarried, may be appointed) be of full age, sound mind, and of some pecuniary responsibility. He is usually nominated by the party in interest who petitions the Court for an inquisition to inquire into the alleged lunacy, drunkenness, etc., of the incapable party. The Court usually appoints as a committee some person who is connected by blood or marriage with the incapable party, and who has some interest in his welfare, though a stranger *may* be appointed.

The commissioners, generally three, a lawyer, a physician, and a laymen, with the aid of a jury, hear and try the question of lunacy, etc., and if they decide that the party is a lunatic, idiot, habitual drunkard, or person incapable of managing his own affairs, a committee is appointed by the Court in which the proceedings were commenced, by its order, duly entered. The committee should provide himself with a certified copy of this order as his authority to act.

The commissioners at the same time ascertain the nature and value of the incapable party's property and estate.

A committee, like a guardian, may be either the committee of the person or property. One person may be committee of the person, and another the committee of the property, but usually the same person is appointed committee of both.

SECTION 72. Bond and Security.—The same provisions of law now (under the new Code) relate to the amount and nature of the security required to be given by a committee as is required of a guardian; for those provisions, see Section 64, under the head of "Guardians." A committee of the *person* must give security where a guardian of the *person* would be required to give it; and a committee of the property, like a guardian of the property, must always execute and file his official bond before he can enter upon the discharge of his duties, and a committee of the person must also execute a bond before he has a right to act, when required to do so by the Court.

SECTION 73. Power and Duties.—"A committee, either of the person or of the property, is subject to the direction and control of the Court by which he was appointed, with respect to the execution of his duties; and he may be suspended, removed, or allowed to resign, in the discretion of the Court. A vacancy created by death, removal, or resignation may be filled by the Court. But a committee of the property cannot alien, mortgage, or otherwise dispose of real property, except to lease it for a term not exceeding five years, without the special direction of the

Court, obtained upon proceedings taken for that purpose." (Code, Section 2339.)

The committee of the person of the lunatic, etc., must carefully watch over him, and see that no harm comes to him; he must do everything he can for the comfort and entertainment of his charge, always with a view of inducing the lunatic's recovery of his senses, if possible; he must see that he is fed and clothed in a manner proportionate to the amount of income from his estate. Frequently in cases of extreme and acute affliction it becomes necessary that the incapable person should be confined in an asylum or hospital devoted to the treatment of persons similarly afflicted. In such cases it is not absolutely necessary that the committee should reside in the same institution, or even in the same city with the lunatic, etc., but he should in the first place personally proceed to the institution, and by inspection of the surroundings and conversation with its officers ascertain and satisfy himself that it is a place where the lunatic will in all respects be well treated.

The committee of the property must carefully keep and preserve it, and deal with it in all respects for the lunatic's interest. He may under direction and *order of the Court* sell the real estate of the lunatic. In such case he must of course account for its proceeds, so he may also be directed to purchase real estate where it is shown to the Court that it will be for the lunatic's interest to do so, and generally any disposition of his property may be made under the direction of the Court for the lunatic's benefit.

The lunatic is primarily to be supported from the *income* of his estate, which the committee should invest in safe securities, as on bond and mortgage on real estate; but where the income may prove insufficient to maintain him, then the principal must be devoted to that purpose.

A committee of the property pays over to the committee of the person the funds necessary for the support of the lunatic.

A committee should have the incapable party placed in an asylum only when necessary, and only on the order of the Court. Where the lunatic's estate is large, the committee may obtain leave of the Court authorizing him to employ a clerk or agent to assist him in the care and management of the estate, and that his compensation be paid out of the fund.

Upon the death of the lunatic, etc., the committee's duties cease, except to pay over to the lunatic's executor (where he made a will when sane) or his administrator all property remaining in his hands, after deducting his expenses, commissions, and the costs of his accounting, but such property should be so transferred *only* upon the order of the Court.

Section 2321 of the Code declares that the Court (through the committee) must preserve the property of such an incompetent person from waste and destruction ; and out of the proceeds thereof must provide for the payment of his debts, and for the safe keeping and maintenance and the education, when required, of the incompetent person and his *family*. A committee possesses the general power to sue and be sued by leave of the Court.

SECTION 74. Commission and Compensation of the Committee.—A committee of the property is entitled to the same compensation as an executor or administrator, and for the compensation and commission to which an executor or administrator is entitled see Section 39, under the head of "Executors and Administrators." But in a special case, where his services exceed those of an executor or administrator, the Court may allow him such an additional compensation for such additional services as it deems just. The compensation of a committee of the *person* must be fixed by the Court, and paid by the committee of the property, if any, out of the funds in his hands.

SECTION 75. Accounting.—A committee of a lunatic or other incompetent person must now, under the Code of Civil Procedure, make and file the same annual account as is required to be filed by a guardian in the Surrogate's Court, and for the purpose of filing such account the committee is deemed a general guardian of the property, and the person for whom he is committee is deemed a ward. The account, etc., must be filed in the office of the clerk of the court by which the committee was appointed, or if he was appointed by the Supreme Court, in the clerk's office where the order appointing him is entered.

That is, the committee of the property must, in the month of January of each year, as long as any of the incompetent party's property, or of the proceeds thereof, remains under his control, file in the clerk's office, as aforesaid : 1. An inventory, containing a full and true statement of all the party's property, and its value, and the manner in which it has been disposed of ; and 2. A full and true account, in form of debtor and creditor, of all his receipts and his disbursements during the preceding year. Annexed to the inventory and account must be an affidavit, by the committee, to the effect they are in all respects true and correct. (For fuller particulars as to the exact facts and items to be set forth in the inventory and account, and the statements to be made in the affidavit, see Section 65, *ante*, under the head of " Guardians.")

INDEX.

Spotted something that isn't quite right?

Let us know and we'll fix it for future reprints.
And as a thank you for your diligence, we'll
send you a free Sothis book of your choice.

publisher@sothis.press

This page intentionally left blank

Made in United States
Orlando, FL
04 November 2026

90207835R10067